TURNING POINTS

TURNING POINTS

STORIES FROM THE TV SHOW
WAKING UP IN AMERICA

A COLLECTION OF ESSAYS AND
INTERVIEWS

TAJCI CAMERON

TURNING POINTS Copyright © 2016 by Tajci Cameron.

All rights reserved. Printed in the United States of America. No part of this book may be used or reproduced in any manner whatsoever without written permission except in the case of brief quotations embodied in critical articles or reviews.

For information contact
tajci.official@gmail.com

Cameron Productions
2020 Fieldstone Parkway Suite 900-249
Franklin, Tennessee 37069
United States of America
(818) 782-0740

www.wakingUPrevolution.com

Book and cover design by
Josip Bosnjak and Tajci Cameron

Cover Photo by Danko Puttar

ISBN: 978-0692628492

First Edition: January 2016

10 9 8 7 6 5 4 3 2 1

*Dedicated to
all who have ever felt stuck.*

CONTENTS

ACKNOWLEDGMENTS   11

ARE YOU LIVING YOUR DREAM
OR SOMEONE ELSE'S?   15

PART ONE

1. THREE PERMISSIONS I GAVE MYSELF AFTER MEETING GLENNON   21
2. WHAT WOULD IT BE LIKE IF FOR ONE DAY YOU JUST DIDN'T COMPLAIN?   25
3. FALLING IN LOVE WITH THE ELDERLY AND REDISCOVERING OUR PURPOSE   29
4. STIRRING THE POT OF SKATEBOARDING MAINSTREAM CULTURE   33
5. WHEN FLYING HIGH NO LONGER SCARES US   38
6. HOW TO ENVISION YOUR TRUE SUCCESS   43

PART TWO

7. HOW ONE MOTHER'S AWAKENING IS INSPIRING OTHERS TO LIVE THEIR FREEDOM   49
8. PERMISSION TO MIND YOUR BUSINESS: GRANTED   53

9. HOW HAVING A BIGGER PURPOSE CAN
   HELP YOU BECOME DEBT-FREE   57
10. TOURING VIRTUALLY: A NEW WAY
    FOR ARTISTS TO REACH THEIR FANS   62
11. HOW FORMER MODEL LORETTA WILGER
    INSPIRES WOMEN TO FEEL BEAUTIFUL   67
12. TWO LIFE LESSONS WE LEARN BEST
    THROUGH EXPERIENCE   72
13. DO OUR PASSIONS DEFINE WHO WE ARE? 77
14. FOLLOWING YOUR OWN PATH WHILE
    KEEPING THE LEGACY   81
15. ONE LESSON I LEARNED FROM THIS
    GUITAR TEACHER (AND IT'S NOT HOW TO PLAY) 85

PART THREE

16. HOW WELDING FIXED MORE THAN METAL   91
17. WHEN YOUR HAIRSTYLIST GIVES YOU
    MORE THAN PRETTY CURLS   96
18. MUSIC, LITERATURE AND EXPANSION   101
19. THE FOODSCAPES OF OUR FUTURE   106
20. WHEN LOVE FINDS US   111
21. WHAT DO YOU DO WITH SMALL
    POCKETS OF TIME?   116
22. WHEN ART SETS US FREE FROM
    FEELING INADEQUATE   121

PART FOUR

23. HOW FORMER NFL RUNNING BACK TIM WORLEY
    FOUND HIS MOST IMPACTFUL GAME 128
24. FINDING HEALING IN 'PORTRAITS IN FAITH' 133
25. HOW VOLUNTEERING CAN HELP
    THE WORLD (AND YOU) 138
26. HOW THIS ONE POET IS GIVING
    A VOICE TO THE VOICELESS 143
27. WHAT THIS STREET FIGHTER TURNED
    WORLD CHAMPION TAUGHT ME 148
28. HOW A LITTLE JAR OF BODY BUTTER
    FROM THISTLE FARMS HEALS EVERY BODY ... 153
29. LOVE THE HOMELESS - LESSONS FROM
    SANDY GRIFFIN 158
30. PEACE WITHOUT UNDERSTANDING 163
31. WAKING UP TO DANCE, MINDFULLY 168

CLOSING

MAKING BIG LIFE SHIFTS: IT'S NOT THAT SCARY
AFTER YOU LEARN A FEW LESSONS FROM THOSE
WHO HAVE DONE IT 175

ALSO BY TAJCI 178
ABOUT THE AUTHOR 179

ACKNOWLEDGMENTS

When I was 13 years old, I wrote an essay for a school project. My teacher asked me to read it out loud in front of the class. I read with such fervor and enthusiasm that everyone laughed at me — except for my teacher, who encouraged me to never stop expressing my thoughts, even when it becomes frightening. I did lose my confidence for a while, and kept quiet. When I had my awakening, her words were among the first things I remembered. My deepest gratitude goes to my Croatian language teacher Pavica, who probably doesn't even know how much she has influenced my life.

This collection of essays was inspired by the amazing people I had the honor to interview on my show *Waking Up in America*. Here are their names (in order of appearance): Glennon Melton, Joe King Kirin, Jana Larkin, Lew Ross, Stowe Dailey, Calvin LeHew, Amber Lilyestrom, Brandy Stanton, Brittain Kovac, James Wassem, Loretta Wilger, Dr. Cary Gannon, Lucinda Ruh, Violet Grgich, David DeLoach, Joe Marolda, Steve Reiner, Chris Katsaropoulous, Dee Worley, Anne Armstrong, Olga Alexeeva, Tim Worley, Daniel Epstein, Megan McInnis, Eric Melton, Rashad thaPoet, Rev. Becca Stevens, Sandy Griffin, Robin Mizaur and Dr. Jamie Marich.

I want to acknowledge *Huffington Post* for giving me the opportunity (and motivation) to deliver an essay each week and publish it on their platform.

My husband Matthew and our three sons Dante, Evan and Blais supported me with tremendous love and patience as I spent long days in my office immersed in my passion of telling stories. They have provided wisdom and inspiration throughout the season. During the summers, Evan doubled as my editor, and Dante and Blais helped with transcribing.

My *Waking Up in America* production partner Stormlight Pictures (Producer Matthew Cameron and DP Logan Christopher), without whom we wouldn't have a show or any interviews.

Finally, my amazing editor MK Cameron whose skills, deep understanding and dedication to our work gave me the confidence to proceed even though English is not my first language.

Who looks outside, dreams;
who looks inside, awakes.
- Carl Jung

ARE YOU LIVING YOUR DREAM OR SOMEONE ELSE'S?

DO YOU DREAM OF DOING SOMETHING GREAT IN YOUR LIFE, something that will leave a mark after you are gone? Do you wish to live the life you are made for, and be remembered for your uniqueness and authenticity?

I hope you are saying "yes!" because that's what we are all called to do. The world is counting on you. For the last decade, I have traveled all over America performing for all kinds of audiences. I've had the privilege to connect with others, hear their stories, see how they've awakened from their discomforts to their purpose and how they discovered the essence of who they are meant to be.

Waking Up in America tells these stories and connects them with music, which I believe has the power to transform.

Our fast-paced, exhausting and demanding world can put us into an overload mode where we just want to "check out."

Sometimes we break down; other times we find ways to function on autopilot. Many of us tend to distract ourselves with work, shopping, social media, smart phones, alcohol, or drugs.

We try different jobs and careers with the hope that we will become successful, loved and powerful enough to change the world we complain about. Instead of feeling accomplished, we feel like we aren't getting anywhere — only spinning our wheels and wasting our lives.

That's when we need to pause, take a breath, and try something completely different.

There are countless stories of people who have made drastic changes in their lives because they felt lost or unfulfilled. People who have found a new sense of purpose along the way to discovering who they were meant to be.

I love exploring those stories and finding the "waking up moments" in their lives, because I've been there myself. Twice in my life, everything seemed to be beautiful, but I was miserable, lonely, and exhausted. Particularly because everyone else was telling me that I "should be happy."

The first big shift in my life came when I left my successful career behind and came to America. I was 21, a superstar in my home country of Croatia, celebrated and adored by millions, and yet I was lost inside. In a moment of courage, I found the strength to start over completely.

'The land of the free and the home of the brave' gave me the ability to discover who I was and stop trying to live a life that would please my fans and managers. I was able to find my own freedom for a while.

But a few years later, I got stuck in what I thought was The American Dream.

I did everything 'right' — I got married, had kids, had faith. The truth was, I was fighting depression, anxiety, and my husband.

I thought of leaving everything behind again, switching continents and starting over. But I realized that doing that earlier hadn't solved my problems. (Plus if I kept it up, I'd eventually run out of continents.) Repeating the same pattern would only yield the same results.

The only other solution was to stay and try to make a change in the one place in the world where I actually could: within myself.

Of course, it wasn't as clear-cut as moving out and getting a new place. The process would take many months, even years. Just like it does to set up a new home, put up pictures, throw out old clutter, and adapt to a new environment after a move.

It all starts with a moment of clarity in which we decide to commit and set our intention to make the change we desire in our lives.

Each one of the stories I explored is different and unique. What they all have in common is a sense of purpose and connection.

The people I talked to had the courage to commit to shifting a belief, a perspective, or an attitude. They found the strength to face something that had been holding them back for too long, preventing them from being who they were meant to be.

Some "waking up moments" are hard — illness, addiction, divorce, death of a loved one — but some are gentle. Like caring for an aging parent, or feeling a firm and steady inward pull toward a new beginning. And this is not a once-in-a-lifetime thing. We need to constantly be tuning into our inner selves, finding ways to change and adapt as we grow and expand within the flow of life itself.

When we do, we no longer get stuck in someone else's expectations of us, or someone else's dream. We discover the joyous and purposeful person we are meant to be. Through showing up with our unique gifts, we create ripples of positive change in the world.

So look around for the inspiration that will trigger your 'waking up moment' — I'm sure you'll find it.

Sometimes we realize it has been there all along, it just takes seeing the world through new eyes in order to recognize it.

What I know for sure is that when you are ready for it, when you open up your heart and say "yes," you'll see that it's always been there waiting for you.

EACH CHAPTER is inspired by a video episode with an interview and a related song. Available for you at WakingUpinAmerica.net (Season 2)

WATCH: Waking Up in America (EP 1)
SONG: "Keep Your Head Up" (Tajci)

PART ONE

Be still and know you are not alone.

ONE

THREE PERMISSIONS I GAVE MYSELF AFTER MEETING GLENNON

Learn to be still. Even in discomfort.

WHAT WAKES YOU UP? What makes you feel most alive and excited to show up in the world as "you" — just the way you are?

And when you feel insecure, what do you hide behind?

When you are scared, lonely or lost, do you try to numb the pain, smile and say "I'm fine," because that's the acceptable thing to do?

Glennon Doyle Melton is the New York Times bestselling author of *Carry On, Warrior*, a HuffPost blogger, and the founder of the exploding online community Momastery.com. On *Waking Up In America* we talk about how becoming a mother was her wake-up call to seek healing from addiction, and about her view that all beautiful things in life come with our ability to sit with the pain.

I hadn't heard about Glennon until my friend, health and wellness coach Ken Fried from Naples, Florida, ran into her. Ken was giving Free Hugs at the local market, when Glennon, being her beautiful self, paused for the opportunity to get a hug and show appreciation for Ken's gift. Upon meeting her he immediately sent me a message that I needed to check out her website and her blog.

Ken and I both believe that we are all connected, and that nothing is a coincidence. So I dove into Glennon's work. I knew there would be something I needed to hear.

DO YOU ALWAYS JUST SMILE AND SAY "I'M FINE"?

I've been pondering those first questions and exploring different answers through my blogs and music for a while.

Glennon's gift is her unapologetic and disarmingly honest self. Here are three permissions I realized Glennon helped me to give myself.

Permission #1 — You don't have to apologize for who you are.

It sounds so simple and obvious, but it's actually not. In Glennon's story, she is a sensitive soul who somehow thought that was a bad thing. Many of us feel that if we don't fit a certain mold we need to apologize for it. I am a social introvert who needs a lot of quiet time. I can't always be "up" and "entertaining." No apology needed. Each of us is made unique and different.

Permission #2 — You don't have to run all the time. Sitting still is okay.

When we have a fever or a flu we rest. Sure we can load up on symptom-relieving medicine, but the illness needs to pass its course. It's the same with emotional pain. Feeling insecure about our pain is okay. Don't run from it. It's all a part of growing. Hiding or numbing ourselves from our pain is not going to help us in the long run. It will only take the pain away for a moment. Sitting still through it, acknowledging it and letting it flow along with the love and grace in our lives helps us to grow and become more of the person we are created to be. In Glennon's words: "Everything is dependent upon our ability to sit with discomfort. And not numb it, and not reject it and not use it to hurt other people... but just sit with pain. Everything beautiful comes from there."

Permission #3 — "I'm scared" is a perfectly acceptable answer.

In her TEDx talk Glennon relates how as a child she was taught that the only appropriate answer to the question "How are you?" is: "I'm fine." I learned that as an adult when I came to America. Initially I was confused, then I too accepted it, until I couldn't pretend any more and I broke. I wrote about my fight with it in a song:

"I saw you at the art show
you looked and smiled at me
you asked how I was doing
but you didn't really want to hear what I had to say
cause I'm not gonna lie
I'm not gonna smile and say: "I'm fine."

Cause I'm tired of weather and I'm
tired of small talk and I'm
tired of kissing air.
And I don't want to fit in this
world that you live in, I just
want to be the way I am."

I encourage you to look into Glennon's work and let her inspire you to awaken to your self, learn to sit still with discomfort instead of numbing it, and live unapologetically as the person you are created to be.

Because when we give these permissions to ourselves we become inspiration for others to do the same.

WATCH: Carry On, Warrior (Glennon Doyle Melton) (EP 2)
LISTEN: "I Feel" (Tajci)

PONDER: Glennon Melton's message is powerful: it's only when we are able to sit with discomfort that we can understand WHY and WHAT we need to shift in our lives in order to move out of it.

APPLY: When you get anxious, lonely, sad or angry, bring your awareness to how it feels in your body and in your heart. Don't push the pain away by taking on a task, or by picking up your smart phone and checking your social media updates. Take a few moments and sit with it. What is revealed to you when you do?

TWO

WHAT WOULD IT BE LIKE IF FOR ONE DAY YOU JUST DIDN'T COMPLAIN?

Unproductive complaining solves nothing

WHAT WOULD IT BE LIKE IF FOR ONE DAY YOU JUST DIDN'T COMPLAIN? If complaining wasn't an option? What would you do? — asked Joe Kirin, founder of the No Complaints Day Challenge when I met with him in Naperville, Illinois.

He showed up wearing a nice suit jacket and a fresh blue and white checkered shirt that set off the blueness of his eyes. Right away I noticed a beautiful bird pin on his lapel that reminded me of my grandmother. Every time she went back to the village where she was born, just outside of Trieste, Italy, she would come back with pins like Joe's. "Povero mio!" I remember Nana repeating to herself on days when things were not going her way. "Was that complaining?" I thought to myself.

I asked him to tell me about the little bird pin.

"It was my mother's," he said. "I always wear it when I dress up."

Joe founded the No Complaints Day Challenge in memory of his mother. When she became very ill, Joe noticed how little she complained about the health challenges that she faced.

Joe's parents were both from Croatia. I asked him if, prior to his mother's illness, his family complained a lot. Not quite intentionally, I found myself complaining about how Croatians always find something to complain about.

"I think we had the same amount of complaining as any family has anywhere else," Joe said kindly.

They lived in Chicago and his parents made sure that Joe, like the other immigrants' children, learned the Croatian language, music, and dances. He fell in love with playing the tamburica — a Croatian instrument that resembles the mandolin — and kept up on all the popular music from the "old country." We both agreed that music is a great way to stop all sorts of complaining.

Joe smiled at me, guarding his excitement and a little bit of nervousness, and told me that he really enjoyed playing my Croatian hit song at his gigs and events. He asked me about my current work.

"Can't complain," I thought, but instead said "Great!"

I paused and wondered: What kind of response is that? "Can't complain." It almost sounds like "I wish I found something to complain about, but right now, sorry, I'm just not coming up with anything." Ah! The mysteries of human expression...

The cameras started rolling, and Joe began to speak passionately about his desire to help people.

"I started to notice the amount of complaining people do on Facebook. They complain about something and then it's there and then it's gone. It doesn't really do anything... it doesn't really change anything. It just, you might say, begets more complaining," Joe said.

We talked about instances in which complaining is useful and constructive, and those when it's not.

There are several no-complaining challenges out there: Will Bowen's 21 days without complaining, Angie Flynn's 30 day challenge... Many people will vouch for the fact that these days spent without complaining have had a positive impact on their lives. Joe's challenge is simple — just one day.

And his four rules are very simple as well:

1. 24 hours straight with no complaints at all.
2. If you complain, get back up, dust yourself off and continue.
3. If you feel a situation really necessitates a complaint then you can make the call to do so — it's your choice. You can then continue on from there.
4. Have FUN because you can't get disqualified.

I thought a lot on the subject of complaining and decided that I'm going to need a whole lot more than one day to become good at giving it up. But even the process of raising my awareness about how much of my thoughts qualify as complaints will be beneficial to both myself and those around me.

So here are my three areas of complaining I'm going to pay special attention to in the future:

Complaining about myself. This has absolutely no use and it's simply a way to get attention. Further, experts say that we are more prone to complain about everyone else and about the world around us if we get into a habit of complaining about ourselves.

Complaining about a service. Unless I get a chance to calmly submit my complaint to a qualified person who can fix the source of my frustration, I'm giving this one up, too. Complaining to someone who can't do anything about it just creates more hurt.

Complaining about my body aches. Sitting at the computer and working for long hours without a break is a choice I make. Why on earth would I then complain when I become stiff and sore? I should expect it, understand it, and either ignore it and keep my mouth shut, or get up once in a while and give my body a break.

Are you up for the challenge?

Joe Kirin is the creator of the No Complaints Day Challenge, a life coach, and an accomplished singer and musician.

WATCH: No Complaints Day Challenge (with Joe Kirin) (EP 3)
LISTEN: "Da te mogu pismom zvati" (By Ivica Badurina)

PONDER: I learned from Joe King Kirin that complaining can only keep us stuck. It becomes an outlet for our desire to change, while in fact we don't do anything about it.

APPLY: Catch yourself complaining about things you can't control, or complaining to the wrong person about something that could be fixed. Can you pause and look for the real source of your discontent?

THREE

FALLING IN LOVE WITH THE ELDERLY AND REDISCOVERING OUR PURPOSE

Sitting in silence with our aging parents makes space for reflection and deep examination of our lives.

WHAT DOES WAKING UP TO THE LIFE WE ARE CREATED TO LIVE have to do with falling in love with the elderly? On first thought, not so much. On second, everything.

Over the past year or so, many new business and life coaches have emerged in response to the global economic crisis and the need to create more opportunities. They engage us with inspirational success stories and provide us with tools to awaken, reconnect with our dreams and build our own thriving lives.

Like Marie Forleo and Brendon Burchard, they are young, radiant, good-looking, successful and powerful. Their energy is contagious, and they are great at articulating what we all want: to live a life that matters in line with what we see as our purpose.

We read their books, watch their videos, and take their courses in eagerness and excitement to start living the life we were made to live.

But sometimes the material we study seems to be incomplete, or is too difficult to understand on our own. We need the assistance of someone who has done it before and who can give us practical examples and personal insights. It's like taking advice from a guide who has already traveled the road we are on — we find out about shortcuts, pitfalls, and roadblocks that we would have had to discover the hard way if we were traveling solo.

Obsessed with youth, high-energy tactics, and the appeal of instant gratification, we tend to forget the importance and the power of the elderly who, like the experienced guides, can offer us a tremendously valuable perspective.

They have already journeyed through life's many phases — peaks and valleys, ups and downs.

Sometimes we might get impatient because their lessons are not concise and articulate, and certainly aren't technologically packaged for us to easily consume while multi-tasking. We can't just plop a wise old sage down on a chair next to the elliptical at our gym and have them tell us stories while we work out. Or turn them on while we sit in traffic to catch some more of their advice.

With the elderly, it's best to match our pace with theirs, without trying to skim through or fast forward. Their descriptions come with a bunch of footnotes and illustrations. Sometimes we even find ourselves thrown off course by a detour, as we face any unpleasant memories that might have been uncovered.

But when we do stop and listen, or even just hold their hand in ours, their wisdom, truth, and love of life can begin to flow and awaken things that we have long forgotten in ourselves. They can help us to uncover the person we were created to be and re-commit to our purpose.

I've known Jana Larkin for several years. She called me one day and said: "I think I have a story for you. I want to talk about end-of-life caregiving. It's been changing my life." Jana offered to share how falling in love with the elderly was transformative in her life, and how it can be in ours, too.

1. Rearranging our schedules to spend time with our aging parents might be hard in the beginning. A lot of us even fear having to rearrange our whole lives to become their caregivers. Sometimes it's not possible to be caregivers for different reasons, but we shouldn't let fear be the reason we don't spend time with those we love.

2. When our routines are shifted, the door is opened for other, deeper changes to occur. Sometimes we realize that we were stuck in the same place for too long, and the change in our regular routine gives us the opportunity to break free of an unnecessary habit or behavior.

3. Facing our parent's mortality we face our own. If we don't run, hide, numb or distract ourselves from the pain that comes with it, it can be a gift — a chance to examine our business, our priorities and our life's goals.

4. Reaching out to family, friends and community for assistance builds stronger bonds. As a caregiver, you learn to ask for help from others and gracefully accept when others offer to give you a hand. It becomes an opportunity to learn how to be strong, vulnerable, and sensitive to the needs of others who find themselves in caregiving roles.

5. Sitting in silence with our aging parents makes space for reflection and deep examination of our lives. The intimate connection provides a beautiful opportunity to continue to discover who we are as a person.

Sometimes this process is hard, bringing with it lots of hurt and pain. It reminds us where we started as children, recalls all the bruises and scars of growing up, and sheds light on where we are now. If we are willing to listen with an open heart, we can know what we need to change as we move forward so that at the end of our lives, we can say, "If I had my life to live over, I'd do the same thing again."

WATCH: Falling in Love with the Elderly (with Jana Larkin) (EP 5)

LISTEN: "If I Had My Life to Live Over" (by Moe Jaffe, Larry Vincent and Henry Tobias)

PONDER: Jana Larkin's life started to shift while she was an end-of-life caretaker to her father-in-law. Spending time with elderly is a gift we often forget we have available.

APPLY: Call your elderly parent or grandparent today and just listen to them. Don't rush through their pauses. Or talk to an elderly person at a store or church. Look them in their eyes. Imagine yourself at their age. Observe how that makes you feel.

FOUR

STIRRING THE POT OF SKATEBOARDING MAINSTREAM CULTURE

Be who you are and don't let culture pressure you into being something you're not.

On a gorgeous and unusually warm January day, I arrive at the Jim Warren skatepark in Franklin, Tennessee to shoot an episode with Lew Ross, a social activist and the founder of Fickle Skateboards.

While the crew sets up the shot, Lew skates with some locals — two young men in their twenties (one a teacher and the other a government agency worker) and a clean-cut high school kid. Lew lives in Northside, a relatively diverse part of Cincinnati, Ohio, where he connects just as easily with skateboarders from all walks of life.

"When you're skateboarding, all the stuff you worry about, how you fit in society — it doesn't matter when we're rolling on skateboards. You could be on the opposite end of the political or social spectrum from me. When we skateboard together, that's not there," he explains.

We cover so many interesting things in our interview that it's impossible for me to edit anything out. So we decide to break it down into two parts, both equally informative and inspiring.

PART 1: STIRRING THE POT

It all comes down to one thing: Be who you are and don't let culture pressure you into being something you're not.

We talk a lot about conformity and the price people are willing to pay to fit in, finding value through the tricks they perform or the clothes they wear, a topic I've been exploring a lot recently.

"I'm passionate about empowering people to dare to be who they are and to skate differently if that's their thing," Lew says. He runs his brand not because he loves wood, but because he loves the people who skateboard.

"Running a skateboard brand is the way that I can reach to the culture and say: Hey kid, you don't need the hat, you don't need the pants, you don't need the right shirt. You are! Whatever you wear is right because it's on you. Your spiritual being, your intellectual being is what is most important."

PART 2: POWER AND LOVE

It's Lew's personal story that, for me, makes what he does so meaningful and impactful. It's one of those stories that seems to be a common thread in society, and that many will find familiar.

But it's a story that has to be repeated over and over, because within it lies a universal need to be loved, heard, accepted, validated, and embraced. It's a story that when ignored can have tragic consequences. Lew speaks at length about his experiences during our interview:

"Martial arts and skateboarding were a big part of how I began to find my way in the world. You know, 12-year-old kid, sensitive, socially maladjusted… I got bullied pretty savagely. So many people have that story and… I got into a really dark place… I got really gnarly 'cause the world is extremely unwelcoming toward organisms like me. People who are sensitive and idealistic really get… they really get the business in the world…"

Self-harm and rage became a real way for Lew to take control. He looked for power in darkness and nihilism until he got 'whiplashed':

"I was extremely ugly. I valued decay and death very highly, like religiously, and became a very, very dark, evil person for a short time. And then I just got whiplashed around. I started to shatter. I started to fall apart. It was too much for me, all this negativity and all this decay in all of this very sincere punk rock nihilistic engagement. I started to fall apart."

His waking up moment came during a talk by Leo Buscaglia that was broadcast on TV.

"I watched a talk by Leo Buscaglia with my mom and I just began to weep. I remember I was weeping uncontrollably and I left the room 'cause, you know, I 'hated' my parents, I didn't wanna talk about it and I didn't wanna have any feelings and I… it was like one week I saw Leo Buscaglia speak on TV and it busted me. I called my Hindu friend up that night and I said, there has to be a god. And I said I discovered it. God has to be love!"

Lew's personal story of waking up to love has been his inspiration and motivation for how he shows up in the world.

"Being exposed to acceptance and love at a baseline level have… it's caused me to sort of file a divorce with this world and its dumb fashion rules and its dumb conformity and its: Oh well, you have to wear this or wear that or look like this or look like that. You have to be cool, or you have to be thin, or you have to be beautiful, or you have to be gay or straight, or black or white..."

Lew is not afraid to be different and controversial. He believes that questioning authority is the only way to find the relevant truth. True to his beginnings in the punk rock movement of independent thinking and independent life choices, Lew is passionate about standing up against misogyny and racism and phobias of any kind — in skateboard parks and in the world.

"If a human community is going to be bigoted about what you're riding in a skatepark, then that community is definitely gonna fall like dominoes when it's time to be bigoted about other things."

Lew Ross is a social activist from Northside in Cincinnati, Ohio and the creator of Fickle Skateboards. Lew crafts each board in his workshop with the intention of encouraging young skaters to be who they are and not force themselves to conform to the ideals of modern skating culture.

WATCH: Stirring the Pot (with Lew Ross) (EP 6) and Power and Love (with Lew Ross) (EP 7)

LISTEN: "I'm Living for Heaven" (Lew Ross)

PONDER: Cultural expectations and pressure can be a big reason why we stay stuck and never wake up to the person we are created to be.

APPLY: Can you find one area in your life where you are conforming to something that is not authentic to you? Perhaps it's trying to be more like the people that surround you (a 'super mom' or a 'sports dad') or adopting the opinions of others before you gain deep understanding on your own. Observe when it happens and then try something different: act from your authentic self.

FIVE

WHEN FLYING HIGH NO LONGER SCARES US

Don't let the fear of heights keep you looking down.

"FOR A LOT OF FOLKS, FLYING HIGH MEANS FREEDOM FROM THE GRAVITY OF FEAR, a chance to explore the blue vastness of life's possibilities, to look at clouds from the other side, and to see with heightened awareness a panoramic view of God's creation... But for some like me, flying can be a scary proposition. It's sad that a fear of heights keeps some of us from getting airborne, from fulfilling our dreams and our life's purpose. Then again, I guess we're not so much afraid of heights as we are of falling."

These are Stowe Dailey's opening words to *Flying High: A True Story of Shared Inspiration*, a book she co-authored with Calvin LeHew.

I'm pulled in from the very beginning. Stowe speaks so honestly about a fear that I recognize within myself, and I immediately connect with her. I trust her to reveal to me the secrets of how to let go of my own fear and fly high.

Over a two-year period, Stowe and her former husband Peter Shockey met with Calvin on Monday mornings to write a book about Calvin's life — about his successes as a young millionaire and city developer, his failures and crashes, and the faith and spirituality he employed to ride through it all like a winner.

Writing about Calvin's experiences and his philosophy on how to rise above adversities, Stowe reflected on her own life. Intertwined with Calvin's stories, she wrote about her own journey - about her hopes and dreams, and about the fears and insecurities that kept preventing her from living the life she was created for.

Then, Stowe was diagnosed with cancer. It brought her tremendous suffering, but it also turned out to be her wake-up call. One that helped her to "move through the fear" and find the courage to "fly high."

"I felt like the sadness that was in me grew into cancer. And said: if you're not gonna live your life, you're gonna lose it," Stowe says. "And I got that in such big way."

A SECOND CHANCE

I meet with Stowe at the house she and Peter had built together. She still lives on the same gorgeous property south of Nashville, but now in a guest house that she moved into after their amicable divorce.

We sit on a comfortable couch and chat before our interview, and I look around and imagine the scenes from her book. I try to imagine her life in this house, in love with Peter, enjoying motherhood after leaving the pressures of her successful songwriting career. I imagine the girls growing up and Stowe sitting at the desk writing *Flying High*, playing the upright piano and longing for her old life of music, but letting fear keep her down in her comfort zone. I recall the passages where Stowe dealt with her cancer diagnosis, and lay in the sun-room thinking she was going to die.

Stowe's eyes twinkle at me and bring me back from my thoughts. I can see how different she is today, sitting on this couch, than she was when she started writing the book. She is not afraid to be herself. She is transformed. She is at last set free from the fear that if she showed her true self she would be judged, rejected and unloved.

"Fear doesn't stop us from dying," she says with a radiant smile. "It stops us from living."

I tell her how it seems like she has truly conquered fear. But she corrects me:

"I still experience fear... I keep setting things up for myself to do that seem fearful and then I show up. And I move into them. It's like, feel the fear and do it anyway. So, it's like I just move through it."

Determined to live, and armed with the prayers and support of her family, Stowe began to recover. She and Calvin finished *Flying High*, which was now richer with Stowe's own experience of rising above adversity.

After her surgery, Stowe returned to writing music, co-writing and performing with her long-time friend and fellow songwriter Karen Taylor Good. Humorous, courageous, and above all herself, Stowe inspires thousands of people through her music and talks.

Toward the end of our conversation, Stowe picks up her guitar and sings "A Second Chance."

"I got a second chance
to laugh and love,
to sing and dance.
And oh, I know
it's a sweet and precious gift,

a second chance to live."

As I listen, I feel a deep desire to laugh, love, sing and dance with her. I want to fly high and experience the abandonment and power she talks about. I, too, want to learn to move through fear, letting love and grace carry me through.

I wonder if I should cut my hair into a pixie cut or get a tattoo. I might.

Today I'm making a decision to find enough courage to just show up as I am. Me. No longer letting fear scare me.

As Stowe says, 'Flying high... it's not just for the birds and the brave. I believe it's what we all are meant to do.'

Stowe Dailey is a published songwriter who has co-written with such legends of country music as Garth Brooks and the group Shenandoah. She is a published author and motivational speaker. Stowe and her co-writer Karen Taylor Good have formed the duo StoweGood to share their messages of hope and recovery with the world.

WATCH: A Second Chance (with Stowe Dailey) (EP 7)

LISTEN: "A Second Chance" (by Stowe Dailey)

PONDER: Stowe's waking up moment came from the suffering, fear and pain caused by cancer. Only when she let go of fear did she begin to heal. Today she is flying high, singing, traveling and smiling with gratitude.

APPLY: What is your biggest fear? Can you identify in which situation it has the strongest grip on you? Next time when that situation happens, try to pause, breathe and acknowledge the fear. Then focus on your breathing and imagine love flowing right next to the fear keeping you safe and alive — with every breath a confirmation of the fact.

SIX

HOW TO ENVISION YOUR TRUE SUCCESS

Redefine success. Or it will redefine you.

WHAT IMAGE COMES TO MIND WHEN YOU THINK OF SUCCESS? Does it look like sunbathing on a yacht in the Bahamas? Or sipping coffee in your spacious and sunny Manhattan apartment? Or running a global business from your laptop on the deck of your Tiny House built at an undisclosed location? Can it look like riding on a tractor with your dog running alongside? Or sitting in the silence deep in the timberlands?

Calvin LeHew, with whom I sat down for an episode of the *Waking Up In America* show, always had a clear image of the success he wanted to achieve for himself. A friend of mine, filmmaker Peter Shockey, formally introduced me to him.

Peter knew I'd be interested in Calvin's waking up moment, the experience that shifted his definition of success. In preparation for our interview, I read *Flying High*, the book Calvin co-wrote with Stowe Dailey that chronicles his life and the lessons he learned. At one point in his life, he found himself asking, like Peggy Lee's song, "Is this all there is?"

He decided that he wanted more than money and fame.

During our interview, it becomes clear to me that Calvin's life is a constant process of awakening moments, together with a constant awareness and faith that "we become what we think." He became aware of the power of the mind, faith and intentions very early in his life.

"I was raised in the Methodist Church there at Hillsborough Leiper's Fork. And I had a lot of Jesus teachings and it was in my subconscious that 'As a man thinketh, so is he.'"

Calvin learned "The Power of Positive Thinking" from Norman Vincent Peale himself, and began teaching it on his own. He wrote down his goal to become a millionaire by the age of 35 and hit the goal two years early.

But Calvin warns that success, as we know it or think we know it, is not what it's all about. "I had wealth, but I wasn't any happier."

When I ask him about the steps to achieve success in our lives, I'm expecting a three-step mantra like the one he kept on his desk for many years: "Conceive, Believe, Achieve," or Dr. Peale's "Picturize, Prayerize, Actualize."

Instead, Calvin mentions the Law of Attraction and the importance of visualizing your goals, but he really emphasizes the importance of going inward.

"Go in silence and be alone... get away from TV, the cell phone, all these mechanical devices... and get as close as possible to nature. Get into the silence and ask: 'What is my mission? What am I to do next? Where am I to go?' And answers do come."

Calvin personally met three presidents, survived five crashes flying his experimental aircraft, became a millionaire at the age of 33, created

Carter's Court in Franklin (the seventh largest tourist attraction in Tennessee) and The Factory at Franklin. He served as member of the board of directors for a number of different organizations. In the end, he said, it's the invisible and the spiritual that he wants more of. Not the physical.

Today he's the member of only one Board of Directors, at the Institute of Noetic Science. And he says that success isn't where we usually think.

"My Uncle Earl in Lebanon, Tennessee had about 20 acres, a cow, some pigs and chickens. I didn't look down on him but I thought I wanna be something more than Uncle Earl. But you know what now? I have a farm out here. I love getting on the tractor with my dog, and doing farm work like Uncle Earl. We don't have to be millionaires or top of the … That's not where it's at. It's being ourselves, feeling comfortable inside, not holding grudges against other people, having love, forgiveness. I can't say any more than that."

I look at Calvin as he speaks and feel a tremendous gratitude towards him.

I want people to hear his message and avoid the disappointment that comes when our efforts are focused on a goal that we don't actually want.

Imagine visualizing an image of success, employing all your power of mind, prayer and faith. You work hard, spending years, decades, even your whole life achieving it and then at the end realize that the image, your vision was not really what you wanted. It doesn't really fulfill you.

To really know what success looks like for you or me, to be able to visualize our perfect image of success, we need first to wake up.

We need to wake up to knowing who we are, what truly defines us, identify our unique gifts and our purpose in this whole picture of life and do our best to truly show up and be present. That's where success is.

That's why we need silence, where we can ask ourselves these questions without the distractions of someone else's definitions and images of success.

Calvin LeHew is a powerhouse entrepreneur and the co-author of Flying High. *His unwavering belief that you 'become what you think about' has motivated his physical, mental and spiritual success and made him an important figure in the revitalization of historic Franklin, Tennessee.*

WATCH: In Every Adversity Lies a Seed of Greatness (with Calvin LeHew) (EP 8)

LISTEN: "Flying High" (by Stowe Dailey)

PONDER: To really know what success looks like for you or me, to be able to visualize our perfect image of success, we need first to wake up. Otherwise we might find ourselves in someone else's definition of success. Calvin became a millionaire two years ahead of his goal, yet he says he wasn't any happier.

APPLY: Think about the time when you bought something you thought you really wanted, but after you made the purchase you were disappointed. What made you buy it in the first place? Can you 'see' what's purely a well marketed image of success and what's true to you?

PART TWO

Be yourself.
Everyone else is already taken.
-Oscar Wilde

SEVEN

HOW ONE MOTHER'S AWAKENING IS INSPIRING OTHERS TO LIVE THEIR FREEDOM

Live from your soul. All else will come into alignment.

I STAND IN THE MIDDLE OF AN ICE RINK AT BOSTON COLLEGE IN HIGH HEELS with my lovely guest, Amber Lilyestrom, having just finished our interview. "Just another day at the office!" she says cheerfully.

We sing "The Star-Spangled Banner" together, and I relish this completely spontaneous, though seemingly odd moment at center ice in the empty Conte Forum.

The freedom, the laughter, the power, the love... it feels energizing and completely liberating.

Amber and I talk about her "Mama Revolution" course that we

discussed in our *Waking Up In America* interview. Truth be told, I wish I'd had access to it (and all the accompanying support) when my kids were toddlers and I struggled to balance my full-time career with being a mom. My biggest challenge was to be the mom that I wanted to be, and not try to fit in with the moms I was surrounded with.

That's why I am drawn to Amber's story and how through her own awakening, she is now inspiring others to live their freedom and align themselves with their truth.

Amber was a successful college athlete who transferred her passion for sports, marketing and teaching into a career as a collegiate athletics marketing administrator. She was climbing the corporate ladder fast, but began to experience a tug inside.

She explains, "I was chained to a job that required me to be there 40-50 hours per week and I didn't have the time or freedom that I wanted in my life to explore the other things: the spiritual part of my life, my true heart's calling and passion, and the writer part of me."

During the Cesarean birth of her daughter, as the anesthesia affected her ability to breathe, Amber felt a sense of surrender, but also an urgency to wake up and live the life she was created for: "I had this moment of surrender where I thought, OK, whatever is gonna happen is gonna happen, but no matter what, when I leave this operating room things are going to change, right? I am going to make a change."

It took some 'scary steps,' as she says, to make the actual change to begin building her new career as a soul-based branding and life coach. But she is doing it!

I watched her interacting with some of her old colleagues at Boston College during our taping, and I could feel excitement, confidence and gratitude exuding from her. She speaks with enthusiasm about the Mama Revolution and the other programs she has created, and

I can sense her passion for serving and empowering others on their journeys.

"I posted a quote today on Facebook, it says: it's impossible to feel present and guilty at the same time. And I think this is really important, specifically for the moms, because you can be sitting at your desk and... feel that pang of guilt creep in, like, oh I really want to be playing with my daughter right now, but you know what? I'm gonna be more present when I play with her because I had my time to do this (work) right now."

The thing Amber is most passionate about sharing with others is this: "You must first give yourself permission to want what you want in your life."

As we wrap up and I say goodbye to Amber, I reflect on her words. Am I giving myself permission to want what I want in my life? I truly think I am. I want to be doing exactly what I'm doing: traveling, helping amazing people like Amber tell their stories, writing, singing and speaking.

I feel alive and present when I do, and not a bit guilty.

Well, most of the time.

On my way to the car, I check my email and find a message from my son's high school that he was absent. I call my mother-in-law, who was with my three boys, and she confirms that he was, in fact, on the bus that morning. I feel an onset of panic and a pang of guilt. "What am I doing giggling on the ice rink in Boston? I should be home instead making sure my children are okay."

I pause to breathe. I bring my awareness inward and calm the voice that is causing my anxiety. I surrender my need for control and I proceed to (somewhat) calmly find out what is happening... reminding myself that if I needed to, I could always catch the next flight home.

Fortunately, it was nothing, a miscommunication, as my son explains to me via text.

I sigh in relief and feel even more grateful for Amber's reminder that when we operate from a soul-based space, it's impossible to feel guilty and present at the same time.

I drive away looking forward to garnering the tools she provides in the "Mama Revolution" course and connecting with other mothers through her Facebook group Live Your Freedom Mastermind. Perhaps I'll see you there?

Amber Lilyestrom is a soul-based branding and business coach, creative entrepreneur and writer. Amber's goal is to help her clients connect with their personal definition of freedom and from there build business that communicate authentic messages and change lives.

WATCH: Live Your Freedom (with Amber Lilyestrom) (EP 9)

PONDER: Amber shifted her life during the Cesarean birth of her daughter, when the anesthesia affected her ability to breathe. She decided to leave her successful corporate job to follow her heart. Today she runs her own business and enjoys spending time with her daughter.

APPLY: If you knew you only had a limited number of days left to live, would you spend your time the same way you are spending now? What changes can you make today to live a more fulfilling life?

EIGHT

PERMISSION TO MIND YOUR BUSINESS: GRANTED

You are your first priority. Because no one else can breathe for you.

"I'M 100 PERCENT SURE I USED THE BIG WHITE PLATTER ON CHRISTMAS!" I repeat for 10th time as my husband looks again through the kitchen cabinets. I get upset, he gets uncomfortable and quiet, I get louder and more determined to find the platter.

I had prepared the food, set the table, bought flowers and candles... but I can't find my platter and I'm falling apart. I NEED that platter.

But of course, it's not about the platter. My mom was supposed to be with us for Easter, but because of some complications her trip got delayed. I haven't seen her in a long time and I miss her. Last week I worked through all of my designated "walking" and "meditation" time slots and so my body aches and my mind is cluttered. It's not about the platter. It's about me and my deeper feelings.

I am acutely aware of all this even as I make my husband look through the boxes in the garage (where he finally finds it, still wrapped from our move BEFORE Christmas). I want to cry, but it's Easter and my kids are ready for the joy and glory that we taught them this particular holiday promises.

I'm human, and I'm messy, and it's going to take a lot more work on self-examination, self-awareness and mindfulness to really be the best version of myself when my platter is missing. Hopefully I can do that before my kids grow up and my husband gives up on me.

Enter Brandy Word Stanton, CEO and program director of Blu Ambition. She is the woman I need right now. She gets to the point and gets things done "quick, fast, and in a hurry." I need to hear her say, "We are human and we are messy," point her finger at me and with her beautiful big brown eyes filled with compassion say, "Mind your own business. Permission granted."

For Brandy, my business is not my singing or my show, it's not my marriage, not anything that I DO. When she says "mind your own business," she means mind YOU.

I sat down with Brandy for our *Waking Up In America* interview, excited to experience in person what I had already gathered from her online presence and her bio: that she is a force. She's beautiful, confident, and unapologetically herself.

Brandy's courage is what inspires me right off the bat. She didn't wait for a major catalyst to decide to make a change in her life. She actually listened to that "pull" inside, what I recognize as a "whisper" in the depths of our soul.

"Your soul is always going to communicate with you whether you realize it or not," she says. "It's always going to try to pull you to where you need to be."

Brandy was raised to work hard, and she did. She had good grades, went to college, became a single mother and after graduating entered the workforce in social services, finding forever families for foster kids. She was good at it, got paid well, and she was making a difference for "precious children," as she calls them with gentleness and caring in her voice. But her soul's pull was strong, and she listened.

And this is where her courage blows me away. She has a child, she lives with a roommate, she can't afford anything better, and yet, she has the courage to honor the whisper in her soul and make a huge leap of faith to change her situation.

"I was 30-something years old and I didn't know who I was ... I needed to meet myself. I needed to become best friends with myself and I realized that nothing else was going to come until I dealt with [my] self."

I get it. Courage is what we need to wake up, to really make the intention to do what's going to be hard and meet ourselves -- the good and the bad, the shadows and the dark corners.

But then what? What comes next?

Self-awareness is where, she says, it's all at. She stopped watching television, stopped "ripping and running" and "going here and there and everywhere," and she "just took care of her" -- mind, body and spirit.

She makes it sound very doable, and not at all trite. "Life is too short," she says again, and I nod in agreement. God knows I am tired of ripping and running and going here and there and everywhere -- like a chicken without a head... or a hostess without a platter.

"If you aren't going to become aware, and accept, and be accountable for where you are and the part you played to get yourself there, and to take that blame from everybody else and have some accountability for yourself, then you're not gonna go any further."

I ask Brandy to sing, because music heals and speaks to our hearts in ways that words alone can never do. She sings "Heroes (We Could Be)" by Alesso, and when I hear the words, "We could be heroes me and you" and see the light in Brandy's eyes, I feel a tug in my soul telling me that where I need to be is here — right here, right now. I decide to listen.

I don't really need a platter. I just need permission to mind my business and take care of me — my mind, my body and my spirit. That, and the permission to remain human... which sometimes also means "messy."

Brandy Word Stanton is a mentor and life strategist. She is currently CEO and Program Director of Blu Ambition where she works with clients to find, develop, and 'mind their business.'

WATCH: Mind Your Business. Start Here. (with Brandy Stanton) **(EP 10)**

PONDER: Before we take care of everything else in our lives, we must know who we are and take care of ourselves - mind, body and spirit. Brandy Stanton woke up to the gentle tugs from her soul.

APPLY: Take some time today to practice self-care in these four areas: physical (stretch, take a walk, dance, exercise); intellectual (read, learn something); emotional (linger in an embrace, observe how you feel, let yourself be moved); and spiritual (meditate, pray, connect with nature). Challenge yourself to make this your daily routine.

NINE

HOW HAVING A BIGGER PURPOSE CAN HELP YOU BECOME DEBT-FREE

Having a bigger "why" can shift us into a life with joy and purpose.

IN OUR LIVES, WE ALMOST ALWAYS HAVE TO DEAL WITH MONEY. Lack of it, plans for it, worries about how best to use it, negotiations for more of it. It's always going to be a consideration, no matter the circumstance.

On the path of waking up from someone else's dream and living the life we are created for, money is definitely one of the factors we encounter and have to deal with. Period.

As Dave Ramsey, financial author, radio host, television personality, and motivational speaker says, "You must gain control over your money or the lack of it will forever control you."

For some of us, it's the fear of money (or the lack of it) that prevents us from getting out of miserable, unhealthy situations. For some it's the debt that we carry that weighs us down.

Instead of letting our money issues paralyze us, we should try to face them head on. The first step is investing time and effort to learn what a healthy relationship with money looks and feels like, how to create wealth and how to manage it.

There is a lot of information available on the subject: great free online content, radio and TV shows, educational and motivational books and e-courses. It's everywhere!

There's so much out there, it's almost like a manifestation of the old saying: "In America the money grows on trees, you just have to stretch and pick it up." (With "money" representing the wealth of information available and "stretch" being the key word...)

"Stretching," of course, requires effort and sometimes pain. That's why some people choose to walk on by, complaining that the tree branches should be lowered or that someone else should shake the money down and make it easier for them.

But those who are willing to stretch can enjoy the fruits that their efforts bring to them. And make a difference in someone else's life.

WAKING UP DEBT-FREE

Brittain Kovac's great-grandmother came from the same small country of Croatia as I did and settled in Strawberry Hill in Kansas City, Kansas. Her family loved the openness of the space, and the opportunity to own and care for land. Their entrepreneurial spirit was passed down to Brittain's dad and to her as well.

They also passed down the sense of responsibility that comes with any such opportunity: the need to give back. When Brittain was around 13, she went on a mission trip to the heart of Jamaica. "It literally changed my life and the direction that I had planned for my future," she says.

"It just really touched me... and then to come back home to everything we have here and to see the disconnect."

Like most of the girls from her social circle, Brittain got herself a credit card for her 18th birthday. She then graduated with student loans and landed a job that would provide her with an exciting lifestyle and promising future, but was also leading her to put herself deeper into debt.

She continued to make regular mission trips to Jamaica, and her connection with the people there became even stronger. There, she was removed from the materialistic lifestyle and the patterns of living set out for her by mainstream culture, and she began to develop a different perspective.

"In 2009, I was in Jamaica on a mission," she explains. "I was... thinking about my future and something in me changed... I said I'm gonna own a house in Jamaica."

She gave herself 20 years to pay off her debt and save enough money to achieve her goal. Here, Dave Ramsey's coaching and lessons in life and money matters came into full effect — she'd listened to him on the radio as a teenager, driving around with her dad, and now decided that she'd take up his challenge to become debt free. He provided a clear map, an actionable guide she could follow.

Brittain explains that she was able to sacrifice many short-term pleasures because she had a well-articulated plan of action and a sense of motivation that was even bigger than herself. "I had a goal to work towards. I had something... a greater purpose to work for."

Only five years later, Brittain took her dad to Nashville, and in an emotional live broadcast of Dave Ramsey's show she revealed that not only had she paid off her student loans, but also the mortgage on the house she had bought in Kansas City.

Today, Brittain is living the life she was created for by traveling the world with purpose. She even found a way to give sleep a purpose when she opened HostelKC, a philanthropic organization that seeks to provide homes for the impoverished in addition to travelers' lodgings in Kansas City.

"For every 300 beds that are booked we are able to build a home in Jamaica for a family in need," she explains.

When I ask her how difficult it was to save all that money, get out of debt, AND start a business at such young age, she is honest. "[It took] tons of sacrifices," she says.

Having a bigger picture and a bigger "why" — her vision of providing homes for families in need — is what fuels Brittain's everyday choices and actions. Her dreams and her efforts to achieve them affect how she shows up in the world, what she creates and all that she gives forward.

Her plans are to open more hostels where sleep has a purpose in Jamaica for mission teams, but she concludes that she wants to leave her path open wide: "I often remind myself... in a struggling time... to let go and let God."

Brittain Kovac calls herself the Chief Nomad at Hostel KC, the place where sleep has a purpose. In her not-so-spare time she runs experiential marketing, works with startups, volunteers, leads missions, explores foreign lands and looks for any new opportunities to enjoy life and serve others.

WATCH: Waking Up Debt-Free (with Brittain Kovac) (EP 11)

LISTEN: "Breathe" (by Tajci)

PONDER: Brittain became debt free motivated by her desire to build homes in Jamaica. She gave up a lifestyle her peers and friends led, but found a deeper fulfillment and empowerment in becoming a social entrepreneur at a young age.

APPLY: Are there any expenses in your life right now that you can reduce? Do your dreams seem impossible because you don't have the money you need? There are many free resources on internet that teach creative and innovative ways to live with less and do more. Find one that resonates with you and start today.

TEN

TOURING VIRTUALLY: A NEW WAY FOR ARTISTS TO REACH THEIR FANS (AND GET PAID)

Jump off cliffs, get out of comfort zones. But always follow peace.

MY KIDS ASK ME WHY I LIKE TO WORK SO MUCH, AND I TELL THEM IT'S BECAUSE I LOVE WHAT I DO. I tell stories — whether it's through music, video, a live event, or the written word — and it's exactly what I always dreamed of doing.

The one thing I like best about my work is when I send it out into the world, and it comes back with even more amazing stories of how it moved people's hearts. So I create more. I give a lot of it away for free (and thanks to many great streaming apps and platforms, I can reach a lot of people globally).

How do I get paid then? How does any musician or artist get paid these days?

For me, it's always been live events. When I was signed with a record label and sold millions of albums, I only got a small percentage of the sales, so concerts were really where my pay came from. But even though it might not seem like it, concerts and performing, as exciting as they are, are hard work.

Recently, I got off the road after touring for 13 years with my husband (our tour manager and my producing partner), our three children and a small crew of musicians. I needed a break, and wanted time to indulge in little things like lazy Saturdays and pajama days. Plus, touring got more and more expensive as my music and our shows grew.

Touring is far too cost-prohibitive for many artists to afford these days, so we look for ways to make a living at home. Those who are also songwriters try to get publishing deals or land a song placement. Others teach and mentor. I like to produce shows/events and perform, which puts me right back where I started — on the road.

That's why I was so excited to meet James Wasem of Gigee.me. I wanted to know the story behind his passion for building online communities and support systems for "next generation touring."

On my way to interview him for *Waking Up in America,* I feel a bit nervous, like one would be when meeting a rock star. James started out dreaming of being a pilot, spent years on the road as a drummer, and now creates amazing live streaming communities to support artists — so to me, he is a "rock star."

When I arrive, I leap over the cords and stands of our set to give him a "nice-to-meet-you" hug and feel like I've known him for years. He is a nice, kind, ripping smart and handsome guy. But above all there is a sense of deep, steady calm radiating from him, even when we talk about stuff he is passionate about — like the music industry today.

James and his wife live in Montana, where he grew up. He talks about his childhood dream of becoming a pilot, and how he used to trace a fighter jet on his snare drum with a magic marker. "I didn't want to forget my dreams, I was like 12 years old," he says with a smile.

He got a full Air Force ROTC scholarship and was all set to achieve his dream, but after only one semester decided something wasn't right.

"In the back of my mind and in my heart I was being pulled in this music direction. [I] was like it is totally irrational, it doesn't make sense. I've got a full scholarship, I know what I'm gonna do twenty years from now."

He chose to leave school and the stability of his prospective career, but felt assured in his decision. "On the inside there was this peace somewhere there. I wasn't sure what it was all about but I knew there was something that I needed to really push through and follow."

He lived a life on the road as a drummer, and learned to appreciate how hard and demanding touring could be. Recognizing how on top of that, independent musicians are expected to be business savvy in order to succeed, James and his friend David Boone decided to create Gigee.me, an online streaming website where artists could connect with their fans and be supported by the people who love them and want them to succeed.

We talk about his passion to build communities, how music is a great connective force, and about the importance of a personal engagement between artists and their fans. Towards the end, he introduces me to a beautiful song by Boone, with whom he has been playing for many years.

"'Taillights' is about experiencing the fullness of life and not worrying about your social status, your economic status, your trials and travails from yesterday. It's living now. It's living with what you have and living a full life with that."

I smile as I think that of course it's available for free on YouTube. But if we want to hear the band play it LIVE — and have a chance to support, chat and interact with them — we'll have to catch them on Gigee.me.

I drive away thinking that James' dream of becoming a pilot really did come true, in a way — he is helping artists soar and achieve heights it would have taken us much longer to reach on our own, if we even could at all.

And one thing he said, I'm holding onto for good — my memento from James, the rock star.

"[You've got to be] jumping off of cliffs and just making these decisions that get you out of your comfort zone ... But you've got to follow that peace, you know."

James Wasem is author of "Great Church Sound" and co-founder and operations director of Gigee.me, an online broadcasting platform.

WATCH: Building Live Streaming Communities (with James Wasem) (EP 12)

LISTEN: "Taillights" (by David Boone)

PONDER: One of the commonalities of all waking up moments is the sense of peace. James left school and the stability of his prospective (and predictable) career because something was 'off.' Today he is connecting people via online platforms he builds and lives with his wife in Montana.

APPLY: In what situations or environments is the sense of peace strongest for you? Can you observe how this 'sense of peace' feels for you in your body, mind and your heart/soul? Now, try to access that same sense of peace in different situations and environments. This awareness creates a practice, so next time you are faced with a decision, you will be able to recognize it easily.

ELEVEN

HOW FORMER MODEL LORETTA WILGER INSPIRES WOMEN TO FEEL BEAUTIFUL

Simply being yourself is enough to be affirmed, wanted, and loved.

NOT TOO LONG AGO, I WAS AT AN EVENT WITH MY 9-YEAR-OLD SON BLAIS. As usual, I had my makeup on. He was looking at me and then out of the blue, he asked: "Mama, why do you wear makeup?"

"Because I like to look pretty," I said.

"Who told you that you were ugly without it?" he asked.

I got silent and thought of the many people who, in some way or another, made me feel ugly without makeup.

I was guilty as well — I had told myself many times how awful I looked without makeup — my eyelashes and my eyebrows blending into the yellowish tone of my skin; my lips not as full as I'd like them to be; my cheeks that never ever get that 'natural' rosy glow.

Around the same time, I met Loretta Wilger while on a shoot of a music video in Chicago. Loretta was a high-end model featured in Italian Vogue, sharing the stage with Cindy Crawford, Iman, and many other top models around the same time I was a teenager looking up to the supermodels and wanting to look like them.

As she did my makeup, she shared with me her modeling experiences — the glamorous and joyous ones as well as the hard moments of self-doubt and feelings of loneliness — most of which I could relate to as I lived a few years as a superstar in my native Croatia. But Loretta also talked about how she turned her life around, found her deeper 'inside' beauty and is now empowering women to feel beautiful.

WHO MADE YOU BELIEVE YOU AREN'T BEAUTIFUL?

"Beautiful!" Loretta said, inspecting my face before she applied any makeup. I felt a surge of tears coming and tickling my nose, which I knew made it turn red. I had been in the spotlight all of my life, always with full makeup on. I almost never felt it was emphasizing my features, only covering them.

Loretta smiled at me with her gentle and beautiful smile, which came not just from the outside but from her heart. And in that instant, I wanted to believe that I was beautiful.

Growing up, I wasn't one of the "pretty" girls — I had broken my front baby teeth and for years I had an "ugly" smile.

As teenagers, my friends and I were often brutal in assessing our bodies — I was the one with huge thighs and thick calves — so different from the models' long and thin legs. At my very first "grown up" gig at a local soccer club, two gorgeous looking coaches approached me and said I had great legs for playing soccer — thick and masculine. (From that moment I never wore flat shoes. Ever!)

The night I became famous, I underwent the biggest transformation in my life — my curls were straightened out and heavy makeup was applied. Everyone gasped at how much I resembled one of the most beautiful women ever — Marilyn Monroe.

"But I'm not Marilyn, I am Tajci," I said in one of the interviews, realizing I was now trapped in this beautiful image that everyone loved, but wasn't really me.

And then there was the "inner" beauty... of which so many talked about in the same breath as they talked about how easily girls can become "dirty."

A few years ago, I explored this subject with my therapist. She said: "To be affirmed, wanted, loved — these are human needs. To realize that these things can come your way by simply being yourself, exactly as you are — that is what you did not know."

But the lesson that simply being yourself is enough to be affirmed, wanted, and loved is the hardest life lesson of all. One that really can't be mastered — because it's something we already know deep within.

We can, however, work on mastering techniques to "unlearn" cultural conditioning and uncover, embrace and live our truth.

Without the awareness that we don't have to look a certain way, behave a certain way, or please our "audience" — whoever our audience happens to be — it's always going to be difficult for us to feel beautiful.

When we start believing that we are "enough," when we claim our "I am," our inner beauty will show up whether or not we wear makeup, whether our eyes are blue or brown, cheeks big or small, skin wrinkled or smooth, lips full or narrow.

And that's what I needed to hear from Loretta exactly at the time when I first met her. But when she finished doing my makeup and I looked at myself in the mirror, I felt too exposed.

I asked to apply a bit more. She listened without judging me. She sensed my insecurity, gave me enough courage and then let me heal at my own pace. She was like the teacher that shows up, gives you the lesson, inspires you with just the way they are, and then leaves you to absorb the lesson further on your own.

About a year later, I returned to Loretta to interview her for *Waking Up in America*. This time I asked her to do a very 'light' makeup for our shoot. She smiled at me and I smiled back with confidence and gratitude.

Loretta IS a super-model to me... A model of a super person who inspires, encourages, heals and empowers.

Loretta Wilger, owner of "Looks" cosmetics applies her experience as a professional high-end model to help women and teens to better themselves and achieve a higher level of self-confidence.

WATCH: Feeling Beautiful Starts Within (with Loretta Wilger) (EP 13)

LISTEN: "Beautiful" (by Christina Aguilera)

PONDER: One of the hardest things to shift from is the cultural definition of beauty. Without the awareness that we don't have to look a certain way, behave a certain way, or please our "audience"-- whoever our audience happens to be — it's always going to be difficult for us to be ourselves.

APPLY: When you wake up in the morning, before you even brush your hair, look at yourself in the mirror. Pause, notice your eyes, your head, your shoulders, your whole body, and with love and without judgement, say out loud to the reflection, "You are beautiful." Then close your eyes, notice your breathing, your heartbeat, your presence of mind and say out loud, "I am beautiful." This way you are acknowledging the miraculous complexity, uniqueness and sacredness of your human existence. Observe how this changes the way you see others during the day.

TWELVE

TWO LIFE LESSONS WE LEARN BEST THROUGH EXPERIENCE

The only thing we can change in a cycle where we control nothing is ourselves.

IF A FAIRY APPEARED IN YOUR LIFE RIGHT NOW and you could have absolutely anything you wanted, where would you be and what would you be doing?

That's a question I love to ask, as almost everybody paints a beautiful picture in response. They'd be on the beach in the Caribbean sipping a cocktail, or looking over Manhattan from their corner office, or even making a family dinner in their brand new kitchen. If you can see it, you can achieve it, right?

We visualize what we want, we break down our dreams into goals, put in the hours, discipline and dedication, and we find ourselves in the beautiful picture we painted.

But what if when we get there, we find that we feel empty, sad or lonely? Because our answer to the question was missing a crucial part

— why?

"It's obvious," some might say. "Because if I got what I wanted, I'd be happy." Sure. Like a child is happy with a new toy for... oh, about a moment.

1. Getting what you want doesn't necessarily mean it will bring you happiness.

This is a lesson that our parents, teachers, and spiritual guides have been trying to pound into our consciousness for ages. It's also constantly challenged by companies that are in the business of selling us their own idea of happiness. It seems that we have to personally experience it to really believe it. Maybe that IS the only real way to learn that lasting happiness is not a result of something we 'get' -- on our own.

So then we attempt to teach the next step, and judging by the first lesson, it's likely you'll have to learn with experience on your own as well.

2. How to transition from what feels incomplete to what feels filled with true joy and purpose.

There is no one way to do this, but there are some elements that are common to all who master this life lesson: emotional pain, the courage to face it, and the clarity of knowledge that this shift won't come from anywhere else but within — there are no magical potions, or fairies.

But it doesn't have to be as hard as it seems, either. Aside from the pain, we all have access to the available tools: courage, awareness, gratitude, compassion and grace.

If we keep our eyes and our hearts open to learn from one another, the whole world can become our classroom. Even that thought alone can create a feeling of wonder and gratitude, and can begin to trigger the shift.

DR. CARY GANNON

Dr. Cary Gannon is a podiatric surgeon and the founder of AILA Cosmetics, and she speaks out about these two life lessons as she makes them a part of her childhood dream to be a healing and inspiring doctor.

"I'm laying everything about my life out there," she says during our *Waking Up in America* interview.

She lived the life from her own 'fairy question': a successful medical practice, a big house in the right location, a handsome husband and two lovely daughters. But she felt off-balance and unhappy.

Cary is a self-described 'over-functioner,' and she kept pushing herself through pain without pause or self-examination until she broke down.

"You might say that I had a mid-life crisis, but I prefer the term 'awakening.' I started eliminating things (and people) in my life that were not healthy for me. Taking care of my body and eliminating toxic ingredients became a priority."

What I love about her story is the connection between her life and the business she founded developing a toxin-free nail care product line.

Nail polish is so much like this 'picture perfect' life we are after — shiny and beautiful on the outside, covering up the nail in its natural state, and sometimes even hiding dirt beneath it.

Her waking up moment was triggered by a situation at her practice where she found herself unable to provide information about a product she was recommending, because the company that produced it wouldn't allow the information to be disclosed.

She felt trapped, and completely out of control. And not just professionally.

"I was looking at the cycle that I was trapped in... and I just realized, I am controlling nothing in the cycle... and the only thing I can change in this cycle is myself. And if I don't personally change within this cycle, then this is how I'm gonna live the rest of my life. And so I basically had to put a stop to everything."

The first step of her change was a trip to a juice bar and a shot of wheatgrass, because she felt that eliminating all the toxic ingredients out of her diet was one thing she did have control over. Then she turned toward her inner life, for just as we have the power to choose what we are willing to put in and on our bodies, we can choose what thoughts we allow to guide our actions and what voices we decide to silence or follow.

She listened. Among other things, Cary let her daughter Aila, who has a sensory processing disorder, teach her how to stop, slow down and take time to just be. (She later named one of her polishes "Five Senses" and gives all proceeds to the SPD Foundation.)

Cary could have continued her pattern of pushing her pain away, distracting and numbing herself in order to preserve the pretty picture. But she asked herself the question 'why,' and in doing so gave herself the ability to truly find the answer. Who does the 'picture perfect' life really serve? Certainly not her — nor her daughters, nor her patients.

The alternative is a life in tune with our deepest desires and free from the luster of pretense. Deep down, isn't that what we all really want?

Dr. Cary Gannon is a podiatric surgeon and the founder of AILA Cosmetics, a luxury collection of nail care products that are free of harmful chemicals. Dr. Gannon inspires women to embrace the idea that beauty should be functional and healthy, and that we don't have to compromise anything to look, feel and be our very best.

WATCH: Good Health Inside and Out (with Dr. Cary Gannon) (EP 14)

PONDER: One of the most powerful realizations is that the only way to affect the world around us, and change the situations we are in, is to make a change within ourselves. Dr. Cary started by removing toxins from her life - what she ate, what she thought and felt.

APPLY: What can you take out of your life right now that you feel is toxic? Is it junk food? Soda? Alcohol? A thought or a phrase you keep repeating? One that sneaks up easily is, "Oh, I'm so stupid," often used when we make a silly mistake. Pick ONE toxic thing and become aware of it. Then eliminate it from your daily routine. See how you feel after about three weeks of living without it.

THIRTEEN

DO OUR PASSIONS DEFINE WHO WE ARE?

Your passion helps you do awesome things. But your passion is not who you are.

IT HAPPENS TO ALL OF US TO A CERTAIN DEGREE — we develop one thing we really love and start identifying with it. It could be our work that we get passionate about, or our children that we lose ourselves in. We lose the sense of who we are apart from that passion.

For high-performing athletes, musicians, artists, and professionals, the focus and discipline needed to achieve the top levels of success is demanding and often utterly overwhelming, leaving very little room for anything else. Sometimes it's puzzling to hear how some of them struggle in their personal lives, and we find ourselves asking how someone so successful could be unhappy. It's hard to accept that the very thing we love to do and identify with could also be detrimental to our well being.

LUCINDA RUH

Lucinda Ruh is one of those generous souls who offers up the story of her life so that we might benefit from the lessons she's learned along the way, and perhaps answer the question of whether our passions define us through her autobiography *Frozen Teardrop — the Tragedy and Triumph of Figure Skating's Queen of Spin*.

I met with Lucinda at her current home in New York to film our *Waking Up in America* interview.

Taking into consideration her status, her accomplishments and her lifestyle, it wouldn't have been unusual for us to have arranged a highly stylized setting for our interview, but instead we sit on the floor in our dresses and heels, surrounded by the paints, easels and playdough with which her twin daughters Angelina and Angelica are creating pictures of the sky, pineapples, mommies, daddies and things only recognizable by the heart of a child. It turns out to be the most perfect, magical and authentic place to be.

Lucinda was a top-level athlete, the world famous "Queen of Spin" celebrated for the longest, fastest, most creative and magical spins on ice. Commentators and journalists called her a "ballerina on ice" and the audience was firmly on her side, giving her standing ovations and booing the judges if her marks were disappointing. For her, it was about more than just the technical side: "For me, every performance was really like a painting. Like I was painting a story..." she says.

She loved to spin, but is quick to explain how much it became her escape, almost like an addiction behind which she kept all that she wasn't able to express, especially given the environments she grew up and trained in.

"[In] the Japanese culture, you don't speak your mind... [or] your feelings. You kind of hide everything. So, I think everything was so stuck inside. When I was spinning I was showing it through my body. But once I couldn't spin, [with] my body collapsing, it was like my body showing that, look, you can't do this anymore and not be Lucinda. You're not living the life of Lucinda."

Her beautiful world-record-setting spins were causing her repetitive mini-concussions which were sending her body into a collapse. She endured great physical pain, and for several years was virtually bedridden. At the same time, she was hurting emotionally because, in order to restore her health, she knew she'd have to let go of the one thing she loved the most, the one thing that had become her identity.

She loved her career, her accomplishments and the mark she made on the figure skating world, but the point came when she knew she needed to make a shift. She needed to identify herself first as Lucinda, not as "the fastest spinner" or "the figure skater."

During recovery, Lucinda came to the realization that the sacrifice wasn't worth losing her life. She had achieved her dream of "doing something nobody else does" and it was time to let go and move on. She chose to stay in the game and continue winning as a whole person — no longer on ice, but in life.

As we talk, I notice that her signature smile which her fans so loved, the one that never left her face on the skating rink, is now even brighter with the joy, gratitude, and awe that come with being a part of creating new life.

"I grew as Lucinda, as the person... and then I found the man, and I have now my love of my life, my two little angels, my two little girls."

She doesn't hide the fact that the transition was hard. But she also says that she is grateful for every step of the way. Holding her daughters close, she smiles her big smile and concludes our piece with the most beautiful thought that uplifts and inspires just like her skating routines did:

"This is totally different and its own miracle in its own way, you know? Everything I think is a miracle in its own way and we've got to appreciate it..."

Lucinda Ruh, the "Queen of Spin," is a two-time National Champion, two-time World Professional Bronze Medalist, Guinness World Record holder for the fastest and longest spinner on ice, and the author of "Frozen Teardrop - The Tragedy and Triumph of Figure Skating's 'Queen of Spin.'" To get the most out of this chapter, I'd recommend viewing some of her past performances: 1999 World Skating Championship and 1999 World Pro in Washington, D.C.

WATCH: Finding Lucinda in the "Queen of Spin" (EP 15)

PONDER: Lucinda loved her career, her accomplishments and the mark she made on the figure skating world, but the point came when she knew she needed to make a shift and be Lucinda first and not just "the fastest spinner" or "the figure skater." Today she lives a joyful life with her husband and their twin daughters.

APPLY: How do you introduce yourself when asked what you do? It probably sounds something like, "I'm a musician. I sing and play piano." But is a "musician" really who you ARE or simply what you do and where your passions, talents, skills and interests are. Bring your awareness to it and observe if you are defining yourself and others by what they do, or who they are.

FOURTEEN

FOLLOWING YOUR OWN PATH WHILE KEEPING THE LEGACY

Balance is meant to hold you in your sweet spot.

"DO YOU WANT ME TO PLAY PIANO BECAUSE YOU WANT ME TO BE LIKE YOU AND CONTINUE YOUR DREAM?" my then-6-year-old son asked me when I refused to let him quit taking piano lessons. I smiled and said, "No, I just want to give you options, in case you find music useful while following your own."

With that answer I knew I was continuing my parents' legacy: they provided me with opportunities, but always left the choice to me.

In a way this was my dream, to raise my children with open paths ahead of them. So, did I just trick them? Or did I happen to find that magic balance that feels infinite?

I reached out to Violet Grgich, the proprietor and vice president of Grgich Hills Estates, an iconic Napa Valley winery founded by her father Mike Grgich, to ask her how it's possible to keep the family legacy while living your own dream.

We met in Chicago for the 35th anniversary celebration of the Great Chicago Chardonnay Showdown which brought a triumphant victory for the Grgich Hills Chardonnay, and her father the title "King of Chardonnay." It was a glorious evening at which Violet received the key to the city of Chicago and read a proclamation signed by Mayor Rahm Emanuel declaring May 7, 2015 as "Great Chicago Chardonnay Showdown Day."

Mike Grgich is a giant, but Violet is clearly not overshadowed by his success; she lets her own soul shine through with much genuine love and gratitude.

When I ask her about her story in our interview for *Waking Up in America,* she starts with an early memory:

"I was told stories about how they were nearly killed, how they had no food to eat, my Dad struggled to come to America to find a land of freedom..."

To every immigrant (and every winemaker) Mike Grgich's journey is tremendously inspiring and empowering. He arrived in America poor but hopeful, and eventually achieved a level of success that placed him on the menus of famous restaurants, the White House wine cellar, in history books and the Smithsonian Museum. The cardboard suitcase he brought with him is displayed there along with a stack of books and his old beret, part of the wine section in the ongoing exhibition 'FOOD: Transforming the American Table 1950-2000.'

"I always remember my father telling me that in America you can achieve whatever you want as long as you have the will and the passion. So when he was growing up in his very small, very poor village in Croatia, he was one of many, many lines of Grgiches... his father told him to every day do your best, every day learn something new, and every day make a friend."

Her father wanted her to take over, but despite his nudging Violet couldn't see herself ever running the business. However, she did take his advice to do her best, learn something new and make friends to heart. Being 'painfully shy,' as she describes herself, she leaned toward literature, science, art and music.

Violet holds a masters degree in music, playing harpsichord and specializing in early baroque music. Her husband is a musician too, and when she talks about music it's with an extra degree of excitement.

So to her, it was a little upsetting when she would be away studying and following her passion, but her father kept asking only when she was coming back home to work at the winery.

I press her further: How does running the winery fit into her dream? It certainly seems now that she is living her own dream...did she have a 'waking up moment' that brought her to where she is now?

She tells me that it happened gradually for her, as she realized "that [the] ability to do everything and learn everything could be combined in this wonderful [family] business."

"I used to love walking on the railroad tracks. And it was so hard at first to find your balance. You sort of bent back and you [fluttered] your arms about, but once you found that point of balance, that point felt infinite. It felt like no matter what direction you lean left or right, front or back it would hold you because it was infinite. Balance is infinite. It will hold you no matter what."

When Violet found that infinite balance, she was able to grow and expand without the fear of falling.

She can continue to learn, play and perform music, run the winery, be a mother, have a marriage, travel around the world, do whatever it is that she wants to do - she can continue her father's dream as a part of her own.

When this balance comes from within, the dreams we follow are no longer under the influence or direction of external expectations, but come instead from the heart:

"Taking time, engaging in the present moment and listening to yourself, that's pretty hard to do. And when you can turn inward, create that quiet space and listen, [your soul] will tell you."

Violet's dreams are clearly free, and entirely her own. And the way she is following her own path while keeping her father's legacy is truly inspiring.

Violet Grgich is the proprietor and vice president of Grgich Hills Estates. In addition, she and her husband Colin Shipman founded Les Violettes, an early baroque 'band,' and regularly perform in concerts and events like Napa Valley Festival del Sole.

WATCH: Balance is All. In Wine and Life (with Violet Grgich) (EP 16)

PONDER: When we find the balance that comes from within, the dreams we follow are no longer under the influence or direction of external expectations, but come instead from the heart.

APPLY: Do a simple exercise that quickly assesses how much time and effort you are putting into different areas of your life that are important to you (family, health, spirituality, career, etc). Are they balanced or is one area dominating? What can you do to correct the imbalance?

FIFTEEN

ONE LESSON I LEARNED FROM THIS GUITAR TEACHER (AND IT'S NOT HOW TO PLAY)

Remember your dreams. When you wake up they bring you back to life.

I REMEMBER THE DAY I WOKE UP WITHOUT A DREAM TO FOLLOW. I was visiting a friend in Maine, staying in a picturesque attic room with a gorgeous view of the mountains. I was filled with joy and awe. I had just turned 22, and all of my dreams had come true.

I'd eaten lunch with royalty (at a Royal Polo Luncheon hosted by Prince Charles and the late Lady Diana), was a superstar (in my home country of Croatia), moved to NYC on my own, learned how to speak English fluently and had gotten a great review for my role in an American musical. I'd also had a profound spiritual experience which opened up my mind, my heart and my soul to be aware of the wonder of all that I'd been given.

All of these, I had dreamed up from a place deep within my heart and they made me feel alive.

But then, my insecurities kicked in and I became afraid that I had been given too much, and that I had used up all of my dreams-come-true passes. I decided to focus on goals and plans instead and worked hard to achieve them. Because I based those on the outside expectations and perceived ideas of a good life, they left me lost and confused, disconnected from who I was created to be.

After having my own awakening, I moved to Nashville to be surrounded by people who aren't afraid to dream big, pursue their dreams and still maintain a stable family life.

MEETING DAVID

While searching for a guitar teacher for my teenage son I ran into David DeLoach, an incredibly talented Nashville musician.

As nothing is a coincidence, David had a lesson for me that I needed to hear. I was deeply moved and asked him to share it on *Waking Up in America*.

David grew up on a military base, and had a path to become an aerospace engineer carved out for him. Instead he became a guitarist, completely immersed into music.

"It was not unusual for me to practice six to eight hours seven days a week. And to gig five or six nights a week... It was a little bit out of balance, to be honest."

He fell in love with an Argentine woman and realized he needed to make some changes in his life. So David quit the one thing he identified with, got a job as a ditch digger and then a full ride scholarship to study theology.

"When they handed me my diploma at the end of it all, I thought... I don't feel any closer to God from all this stuff I'd learned in my head."

He ended up working for a bank and built himself a successful career in the corporate technology world.

One day, David took his daughter to a routine check-up and collapsed in the doctor's office.

"I got dizzy, my chest got tight, had trouble breathing and I felt like the life was leaving my body... I thought, this is it!... I'm dying."

As the doctors and nurses worked to bring him back to consciousness, David had some incredible dreams.

"I woke up on the floor, and I was... like I'd been laying on a mountain stream... just felt like a clear water had been running through me, I felt so wonderful."

For months he tried to remember what those dreams were that made him feel so refreshed and full of life... until he heard the answer:

"God told me. Those incredible dreams I couldn't remember were the Incredible Dreams That I Couldn't Remember. It was the dreams of my youth that I had forgotten. Of being a musician. And I instantly understood: those dreams will bring you back to life."

David didn't quit his day job, but he did pick up his guitar. He found himself practicing late into the night realizing that he couldn't compare himself to others. Nashville was full of brilliant musicians.

So he embraced what was unique about him and decided to enjoy it in a way that brought him fulfillment, authentically and without fear. He developed a teaching style and wrote and published *Play Skillfully*, a comprehensive guitar book which was used at the Berklee College of Music in Boston.

"When you know who you are, it helps you make decisions. You come to a fork in the road and it helps you know which way to go."

One door kept opening after another and David found himself playing with more and more amazing musicians, including a big band jazz group and the Nashville symphony orchestra.

THE LESSON DAVID TAUGHT ME

His smile is contagious and so radiant, it makes me feel alive as I talk to him. "Those dreams will bring you back to life," David says. I nod and let my heart open a little bit wider.

Why be afraid to listen?

Remember the incredible dreams you've let yourself forget and then wake up to make them come true.

David DeLoach is an incredibly talented musician and author of Play Skillfully. *He lives and teaches in Franklin, Tennessee, but with his free online guitar lessons he's been reaching millions around the globe.*

WATCH: Dreams We Can't Remember (with David DeLoach) (EP 17)

LISTEN: "Will the Circle Be Unbroken" (by Charles Gabriel and Ada Habershon)

PONDER: David had a dream that triggered his awakening.

APPLY: What other stories do you know in which dreams triggered people's actions? Do you have a dream you no longer dare to dream? What would happen if you did?

PART THREE

Change the template to create a different picture.

SIXTEEN

HOW WELDING FIXED MORE THAN METAL

You get broken down and rebuilt the way you are supposed to be.

"LIFE'S KIND OF LIKE A JIGSAW PUZZLE — you throw out all the pieces and it looks like, what a mess! But the further down the road you get, the more pieces interconnect and you start to see a good picture starting to form," said guitarist and educator David DeLoach in one of my episodes of *Waking Up in America*.

What's really cool about the puzzle of our life is that it's not two-dimensional — the pieces also interconnect with other pictures, other lives, and people we meet on our path — whether they stay or only pass through. We can never be quite sure where the crucial, completing piece will come from.

That's why the best advice I ever got was to listen and keep my eyes and heart open; to be as alert and as awake as possible.

Most of us look to teachers and experts when we have missing pieces in our lives, failing to recognize when they are filled in from everyday people — regardless of what they do or what authority they have.

And yet the lessons and the puzzle pieces are everywhere.

A few years ago, I was performing a Christmas concert in Minotola, New Jersey when I met Joe, the local "welder guy." I was grateful to Joe for fixing my microphone stands and the step of our van, but I don't think I fully appreciated him until when, at the end of the concert, he presented me with a piece of art he had welded for me and I paused to look into his brown eyes. I caught a glimpse of his beautiful soul that longed to give, serve, and love that was freely shining through, and I sensed he had a puzzle piece for me.

I traveled back to New Jersey, to interview Joe for my show, and while there I got a deeper understanding of the shift in life he had made from commercial welder to metal artist. As a welder, he was detached from his dreams and his passion. He learned that to find his true self and purpose he had to first detach from something else: the toys and the lifestyle he has always known.

Joe never thought of himself as an artist. He didn't think much of who he was, or what his dreams were. He didn't go to college and ended up working on the family farm, as he says: helping his dad and uncle to live their dreams.

Even when in his 20s he started his own welding business and experienced success, he wasn't happy. Still he played the cards he was given and did his best to fill the role he was given to play.

Joe's always had a passion for creating, building, and fixing. His first words, he tells me, were "me help." So whenever his friends asked him to fix things, Joe thrived. He was driven by love and romance to make his first piece of art as a gift for his girlfriend. Soon after that, a friend asked him to make something for a fundraiser. Then another for a charity auction. For the first time, Joe's talent and his giving heart were not only recognized, but acknowledged and needed. He felt encouraged, but still he held back. His commercial business provided not only financial security but also a place where he could hide.

WAKING UP

As is the case with most of us, it's external situations that push us into looking deep inside ourselves and deciding to make changes within. Some people will say that's how God gets our attention.

So, a crisis hit Joe's business, jobs became scarce, and his dad sold the family property.

Just like the metal he cuts in preparation for welding, his life fell apart.

"I feel like I was broken down and rebuilt the way I'm supposed to be," he explains.

Joe had to detach himself from his "big toys" and everything else that was holding him back and still providing him with a sense of security — his comfort zone.

His faith was tested and he was asked to trust, to leave his boat at the shore and align his path with the purpose he was created for — to serve, help, inspire and give without being afraid of being who he is meant to be.

He sold everything and began to create art full-time.

"Starting at nothing again really put everything in perspective. It gave me a chance to have a clean slate and I really do believe that ... the push was really what helped me get to where I'm at right now."

Joe gives a lot of credit to his friends who provided him with support and who believed in him when he was "getting rebuilt" — the process through which he learned to trust, both himself and God.

"I'm getting happier every day," says Joe and smiles with so much emotion, I tear up. I sense how much courage it's taken him to fully embrace the beautiful soul that he is and accept the gifts he has been given, through which he is most powerfully contributing to the world.

Every piece of functional metal art he sends out or donates through his company Vin Art has a "piece of his heart and soul" in it. He is dedicated to his Italian heritage of sharing good things in life — beauty, love, friendship, faith, joy and music.

These are the pieces of the puzzle he delivers to me and so many others who find ourselves moved and touched by his art and his friendship. And it's more than metal that Joe welds into our lives.

"You have to really take a step back from your life first, and look at where you're at and ask yourself is this where I wanna be? Because too many people get caught up and it's hard to detach at at that point. But it's not impossible. Everyone can change their life and make a difference."

Joe Marolda is a metal artist. Passionate about his faith, friends and his Italian heritage, Joe puts his heart and soul into every piece of functional art he sends out or donates.

WATCH: How Welding Fixed More Than Metal (with Joe Marolda) (EP 18)

LISTEN: "Where I Belong" written by Cory Asbury

PONDER: Through a series of struggles, Joe shifted his welding family business into making metal art and in the process he found who he really was — a compassionate man dedicated to his faith, family and friends.

APPLY: Are you hiding any creative talents because of insecurity or a lack of time to pursue them? Clear your schedule this weekend and create something for you. You don't have to show it to anyone if you don't want to, but you also might end up with a really nice gift for someone special. Observe how this process makes you feel.
_____

SEVENTEEN

WHEN YOUR HAIRSTYLIST GIVES YOU MORE THAN PRETTY CURLS

Helping others helps us get out of our old patterns.

"MEN MARRY WOMEN HOPING THEY WILL NEVER CHANGE. WOMEN MARRY MEN HOPING THEY WILL." My husband brings up Einstein's quote as we sit on the kitchen floor and talk about love languages, misunderstandings and our mutual desire to make our relationship better.

"I'm not sure that quote works for me any more," I say, slightly irritated. For a moment a vision of my glowing, transformed self says with a gentle smile, "Nothing in nature exists without a constant change," and kisses him with love and acceptance.

Instead, my real self falls into the pit of my old behavioral patterns like impatience and impulsiveness and I say words that are neither calm nor profound. In that pit, I am back to where I was fifteen years ago when we met, with the exception that I am now able to recognize it. Thank you mindfulness and awareness, goodbye; "Ignorance is bliss!"

The pit's like quicksand, pulling me downward fast. It's filled with gremlins screaming old messages at me, the loudest of them laughing: "Who do you think you are? You can never change! You'll always be the difficult person no one can live with."

I need to stop this vicious train of thought fast, or I'll blow up. Thankfully my husband is tired of talking and is happy to wrap things up.

I turn to one thing that I know works for me. I focus on my breathing, picturing grace flowing in and lifting me up with every inhaled breath while impatience and desperation flow out with every exhale.

This interchange of grace and surrender works to build a stairway out of the darkness. A stairway to heaven really, because it's taking me away from my immediate situation and reconnecting me with the immense Love that holds all of the universe together, me included. I breathe a quick prayer of gratitude.

But that only takes a moment, after which I need all the support and inspiration that's available to help me continue my transformation. Because these pits are everywhere, and change is hard.

I need someone good after this particular stint. Someone who has dealt with repeating old behavioral patterns and who has found a way to shift out of them. Steve Reiner comes to mind right away.

STEVE

Steve is a hair designer whom I first met when I was shooting a music video in Naperville, Illinois. (Aren't hairstylists often great for therapy?)

My attention was caught by the juxtaposition between Steve's tough, tattooed look and the gentle way he spoke and wrapped my hair around the curling iron. I had a hunch he had a story filled with good life lessons. Luckily, he generously shared it with me and on my show *Waking Up in America*.

Steve was a talented, creative kid who went to college to become an architect when a summer job at a construction company turned into a successful career.

"I took some time to make some money to go back to school and just started making so much money, I never went back."

He climbed the ladder fast, and soon became the head guy who worked and played hard, having fun and drinking with the best of them. He married a hair stylist who awakened his creative side and decided to quit his job and go to beauty school.

Steve and his wife opened a high-end salon and bought a big house on the right side of town, but before the paint was dry he was given divorce papers. Shocked, Steve slipped back into his old habits of working hard and playing harder.

"When you are in a boat, and you are flying across the lake, you got this big wake behind you. When you stop that boat really fast, that wake comes and hits you. That was kind of what happened to me."

Steve found himself in a mess he couldn't recover from, not on his own. He sought help and was put on medication. He gave up his salon and got a station at a much less competitive place.

And then the real change happened.

A friend asked him to volunteer at a homeless shelter and a recovery home.

"One of the things that I was missing... was helping other people... seeing what they are going through, and then seeing what I was going through was like, Pffff! Seriously?"

Helping others helped Steve to get out of his old patterns and gain a new perspective on life.

He is comfortable being himself: riding his Harley to work, where he curls and blow dries, cuts and smooths. With a few of his buddies he founded a program called Halfway Hair and on many Sundays he can be found doing hair for teenagers in addiction recovery.

"Sounds like church," I said in our interview. "Showing up where you are needed."

"Yeah! Just like church." Steve responded with excitement. There he found his purpose: to serve and fix more than hair.

BACK HOME

"Insanity: doing the same thing over and over again and expecting different results," I say to my husband a few days after our kitchen conversation. "Did you know that's an Einstein quote, too?"

"By learning to break our behavioral patterns that cause us to react destructively we shift toward being the best version of ourselves. We change. And that's something a man can't wish their wife wouldn't do... Or wife make her husband do," I gently offer as a clarification.

"It's a gift to have each other when we are dealing with our own pits and gremlins. To know that we won't be judged, only loved for who we are — as we grow, transform and expand." I smile at him. He looks at me, relieved that all was well. But he also doesn't feel like talking about it any more.

I grab my purse and I'm off to get a quick blow dry with my Nashville therapist. I mean, hairstylist.

Steve Reiner is a hair designer and a passionate biker who co-founded Halfway Hair, an organization that empowers teens in rehab to regain their self-confidence one strand at a time.

WATCH: Concrete, Curls and Harleys (with Steve Reiner) (EP 19)
LISTEN: "Sunny Day" (by Tajci)

PONDER: Many people get stuck — taking some time off school to make money and never going back because the job becomes a great source of income and power. But going down the path that's not authentically ours can lead to destruction. Even after shifting into a more authentic career, we need to find what really brings us peace and fulfillment.

APPLY: Without switching your career or quitting your job, can you find the peace and fulfillment through using your gifts and talents in volunteering?

EIGHTEEN

MUSIC, LITERATURE AND EXPANSION

Literature opens up your mind and can trigger an awakening.

MY 12-YEAR-OLD SON INSTALLED A STAR-GAZING APP ON OUR PHONES and arranged a 21st century star-gazing family experience. The night wasn't particularly clear and we were sitting in our backyard, which was polluted by the artificial light of our suburb.

But our little devices showed stars and distant universes we could never see with our naked eye. We were able to step outside of our 12-inch viewing space and allow ourselves to look further; it was like having a portal into a space we don't usually have access to.

For me, just as exciting as looking at the stars was watching my kids' thoughts expand into the vastness of everything. The star-gazing (and this little app) triggered all kinds of worlds my kids wanted to talk about — from concepts of time and space, the physics of light and sound, life, God... Every thought, every subject led into another one, pulling us deeper, engaging us emotionally and making us all aware of the connection to something much bigger than ourselves, our little backyard and our smart devices.

I felt grateful that my kids felt free and open to what really turned out to be a spiritual experience.

MUSIC, ART AND LITERATURE TO EXPAND OUR MIND

Growing up, I didn't feel like I had that kind of freedom. There always seemed to be a 'wrong way' to think. I remember wise grown-ups telling me not to think too much about the universe because it was so vast and incomprehensible, it would drive me insane. There were science teachers who discouraged me from making too many connections, and religious guardians who tried to protect me from the dark side that would corrupt my soul if I opened the door too wide. But there was music in my life, which provided an unspoken connection to the divine. And my 7th grade literature teacher, who understood me when the others laughed at me for delivering a very interpretative book report.

So maybe she's the reason literature remained one place in my life where I felt free and unafraid to explore spiritual and alternative realities, where I let my thoughts wander unrestricted, asking questions and exploring possibilities - not just accepting the straight and definite answers.

Recently, a friend of mine sent me a book she thought I'd enjoy — *Entrevoir* by Chris Katsaropoulous.

After reading the first few pages of his book, I called Chris to ask him if he would be on my show *Waking Up in America*. "Your book reminds me of *The Little Prince*," I said immediately. They are two very different books but for me they are both triggers — giving the reader permission to open up their mind.

"I want to know where his spiritual fiction comes from," I told my friend before my trip to meet Chris.

Like many amazing spiritual people I've met on my travels, there's nothing on the outside that showcases his expansive creativity. He lives in a suburb of Indianapolis, and the only difference I noticed when we pulled in front of his house was that his front lawn was spotted with bright yellow dandelions — welcomed to grow free, instead of being proclaimed intruders and expelled from the uniform look of the weed-free subdivision.

His wife is also a writer, so their home is filled with quotes and books and comfortable reading chairs. There is an upright piano in the sitting room where Chris and I talked; he is self-taught and music is a hobby that he also often incorporates into his novels. When he played Rachmaninoff's piano concerto for me, I admired his freedom in doing so, because as a classically trained pianist, I always limited myself to pieces that my teachers deemed appropriate and 'safe' for me.

We talked about expanding our minds, and the importance of art in our lives, and his views on the freedom it opens us to:

"I think there is a lot of programming in our day to day lives. We have certain schedules, certain work obligations, certain programming that comes to us from television, or whatever media that we are [consuming.] So anything that gets us outside of those structures... can help to open awareness. And art, whether it's music or poetry or a novel [can do that]."

Chris has always been a writer, mostly of novels and poetry.

He was writing a thriller novel when his research led him to Glastonbury, England and the Hagia Sophia in Istanbul.

"[Glastonbury] is a sacred place, and on the top of that hill... I had a big awakening experience there... It's a very sacred place... Something just came through me and I started having out of body experiences and past life experiences and all sorts of multi-dimensional experiences, that have gone into making my novels and my poetry since then."

I asked Chris if he was ever afraid of how people would react to these experiences he is writing about. "No," he says, "Because it feels totally natural."

"Everyone is spiritual. Everyone is a spiritual being. Our modern world is very results-oriented, very time-oriented, very structured and those things are very left-brain kinds of things. And so we shut off the right brain, the holistic, the creative in a lot of senses to function in the world that we have."

We are becoming detached from our spirituality. We don't understand it... and a lot of people fear it... maybe because it feels safer to stay within what's familiar.

"When we remember the wholeness of everything, and the connection with the spirit and its source, then we go back to the highest state, and this is everyone's true state as a spiritual being. But it's scary to go back and realize, because people like their own limitations. To know that you're truly a powerful spiritual being opens you up to all sorts of possibilities..."

When we open up our mind and let go of fear, we can begin to explore the worlds beyond our own, the thoughts beyond those we are taught to think, the feelings we don't even recognize because we haven't allowed ourselves to feel. When we expand our consciousness we begin to experience our lives not from the side-lines, but as active participants.

We might even feel as free as children, to look at the stars and grasp the idea of how vast and yet connected all creation is... without any fear that it might drive us insane. Or feel free to paint a picture, or play Rachmaninoff despite the voices that tell us it's not appropriate or safe.

Chris Katsaropoulos is the critically acclaimed author of more than a dozen books, including Antiphony and Entrevoir available on Amazon.com

---

WATCH: Novels that Expand Your Mind (with Chris Katsaropoulous) (EP 20)

LISTEN: S. RACHMANINOV "Rhapsody on the theme by Paganini" (performed by Chris)

PONDER: Busy family schedules, work, and entertainment we are offered through the media can lead us away from exploring who we are and what our purpose is. Art, music and literature can help to get us out of that stuck place.

APPLY: What would happen if instead of watching a movie, you sit in a chair and without doing anything else listen to an entire piano concerto, or another piece of classical music? Or if you visited a museum and looked at only a few pieces of art, absorbing all that it has to offer? Or if you read one poem and wrote down the thoughts it triggered?

NINETEEN

THE FOODSCAPES OF OUR FUTURE

Connecting with nature helps us heal.

"TAKE A BREAK FROM YOUR SCREENS AND COME HELP ME MOVE SOME DIRT," I say to my three boys. They oblige without fuss, each according to their age and personality. My 9-year-old excitedly runs outside, asking for a shovel; my 12-year-old offers suggestions on how to tackle this task in the most efficient way, and my teenager shows up with his headphones on, intending to help do the work but not wanting to interrupt his audio book.

My husband isn't in town when the dirt is delivered, but he built the frames and tilled the soil before he left so all we have to do is fill it. "Not a problem," I say, feeling very earthy and strong.

I've planted herb gardens before — mostly rosemary and lavender in nice pots — and what I had imagined "moving dirt" would look like was something you'd see in a *Real Simple* magazine. You know, with the blue wheelbarrow, red watering can and me wearing lime green gloves, a pretty hat, a flowery dress and a big healthy smile.

But then Jeremy pulls up with a trailer of dirt. It's a BIG pile of dirt. It has a strong odor, and it's full of bugs. He hands out shovels to my boys, who in turn look at me and ask if I plan on paying them for this "extra" chore. "I'm giving you a chance to reconnect with your food," I reply, and get to my job of pushing the wheelbarrow between the trailer and the backyard. Without gloves, a hat or flowery dress.

The healthy smile, however, forms itself on my face during that first load. Throughout the whole process of building, planting and tending my garden, I notice how it stays there and spreads joy all over me, like the vines of my yellow squash and cucumber plants.

As a "city girl," I've always loved farmers' markets, fresh food, and the fragrance of my potted plants. Growing food was something I never thought I'd attempt.

"I'll sing for the farmers and they'll give me food in return," I tell my husband when we play his favorite game, "what-would-you-do-if-the-world-collapses."

But then we moved to Franklin, Tennessee. Perhaps it was the weather, or my neighbors, but I suddenly felt the desire to grow food. Plus, my mom is visiting for the summer and I feel like my boys need an extended chance to play in the dirt and spend some time with her. I asked around for help with setting up some raised beds and was connected with Jeremy Lekich.

During our first phone conversation, he was eager to share with me the motivation behind his work, so I asked him to be my guest on *Waking Up in America*.

I step out of my car wearing heels and a little black dress, sipping my Saturday morning latte when Jeremy arrives in his work truck. "Should I change?" he asks, looking at me. "No, you look great!" I say, secretly wishing I could look as cool as he did in a straw hat and a brown T-shirt.

JEREMY LEKICH

"I grew up in suburban America, played a lot of video games, went to public school, and just sat in a classroom for hours on end..."

There was nothing "wrong" with Jeremy. He was a regular kid with good grades. But when he talks about the video games, I feel a little panicky. This is what my sons will say in a few years, I think to myself.

"I think about how if I spent those hours doing something, like learning carpentry or playing music, I would be an amazing carpenter or an amazing musician, but you know, I beat a couple of video games..."

He chose to go to a working college in the forested hills of western North Carolina because he felt he had been cooped up in classrooms for too long. He loved nature and he was happy working on the landscaping team.

But then, he noticed just how unhappy he actually was — even though he was pursuing what he thought would be his career as a bio-chemical engineer.

"Going to class... I'd be in laboratory and I'd be around all these machines, and I'd be like, ooh... I don't know if I can do this... Because I loved getting my hands dirty, I loved having the sun on my skin, and I loved feeling the wind blow, I loved hearing the birds chirping and singing..."

Switching his majors and choosing a different career was a turbulent journey for Jeremy, but he sought the help of campus therapists and talked it through until he had the clarity to make the most important choice of his life: to follow his own path.

"As I pushed through, I realized I needed to shed the ideas of what society said I should be, and I just had to be myself."

Being himself, Jeremy comes alive. He radiates with joy when he talks about plants, birds, trees and playing music.

He has been helping clients to grow abundant gardens, to reconnect with their food sources, with nature and ultimately with their own purpose. We talk about the healing that this process of reconnecting can bring, and he tells me about the therapeutic garden he helped set up at the Fort Campbell Military Base.

"... Growing food and being around an abundant place full of flowers and scents and life and butterflies and bees, and birds... helps us heal from ... depression, anxiety, or from post-traumatic stress from war."

Jeremy helps me to buy good dirt and quality plants (or seeds) and tells me to have confidence because nature is set to thrive, not fail. It makes sense. Life is like that. When we trust, life expands. When we try to force it to behave our way, it is bound to fall apart.

ABUNDANCE

"Wow! I can't believe we grew this in our garden!" my 12-year-old exclaims when I harvest our first zucchini. "It even looks better than the ones we buy at the store," my youngest chimes in. The oldest smiles at me, understanding the simple and yet most elemental joy that comes from reconnecting with our food, with nature, and ultimately with the Source of all life.

I send out a ripple of gratitude to Jeremy, who has helped my family to wake up and smell the zucchini.

Jeremy Lekich is a landscape and foodscape designer and the owner of Nashville Foodscapes. He also has a band — Turnip the Beat.

WATCH: From Video Games to Foodscapes (with Jeremy Lekich) (EP 21)

LISTEN: Instrumental by Turnip the Beat

PONDER: Nature transforms constantly. It's a great teacher of making shifts and embracing change.

APPLY: Go outside. Find a batch of dirt (hopefully you can find a piece of untreated earth). Take off your shoes and stand on it. Move your toes and observe how the soil feels. Is it hard, wet, cold, soft? Touch the bark on a tree, move the tips of your fingers through the leaves of a plant. What transformations can you identify right there?

TWENTY

WHEN LOVE FINDS US

Let go of the longing for love to 'find you.' Instead embrace that it's already there within you..

I REMEMBER THE FIRST TIME I HEARD GERSHWIN'S BEAUTIFUL JAZZ STANDARD "SOMEONE TO WATCH OVER ME." Its melody reflected my longing for someone to find me and love me and watch over me forever.

It sounded perfect, echoing what I already knew from fairy tales — that Prince Charming rescues the Princess and adores her happily ever after.

It took me awhile to wake up from my enchanted sleep and understand that I was way off with this love thing.

The first misconception was that love would be something a man would bring to me, along with the magic, trust, security and most importantly the sense that I mattered to him. I'd just have to sit pretty and respond when it happened. For a while, I did that.

At first it seemed feasible, because the magic was undeniably there. And it felt great! At least in the beginning. The trust, the feeling of security and the sense that I mattered were arguably more or less there, and yet sometimes completely absent.

When I expressed my disillusionment, someone told me that men can't deliver this love — that it can only come from God. That, too, seemed perfect. I thought that God would bring me magic, trust, security and that I'd matter to him. (I didn't really like the fact that God was a man again, but I let it go... I really wanted love to be brought to me.)

So I sat pretty and waited. And I experienced a few incredible moments in which I encountered God.

God felt very loving. But also so powerful and huge that I almost ran away (like I would from a guy who was way too handsome and way too nice and who treated me in a way that was just too good to be true.)

I didn't run, but I also felt incredibly unworthy and incapable of receiving and living with such love.

That's when I became lonely, depressed and scared. If I wasn't happy with God's love for me, then maybe there was no hope for me. Maybe I simply couldn't be found by love.

The moment I let go of this concept that some remote love would come to me (in the form of a man), I felt it. It surfaced from deep within me and completely caught me off guard.

It asked me, What would happen if you loved YOU?

I felt like Dorothy when the Great Oz told her she had the ability to go home all along — she just had to click the ruby red slippers that were already on her feet.

When love finds us, it doesn't feel like a first kiss, but rather more like that incredible combination of feeling both confident and humbled at the same time. When we finally look beyond our reflection in the mirror and see the beautiful inner soul that's created with and capable of love, we can begin to understand that we belong to the love that's simply always been there — from the beginning of time. The love in which we matter, in which we can trust and feel completely secure, and which is magical not just in the beginning but more and more each day as our familiarity with it deepens and matures.

In that love, we find ourselves. And each other.

DEE WORLEY

I reached out to Dee to ask if I could interview her husband Tim Worley (former NFL player and motivational coach) for my *Waking Up in America* show.

As my husband and producer Matthew Cameron coordinated the shoot with Dee, he asked how the two met. What unfolded was an incredible love story I had to share.

Dee always knew she was a gymnast. She followed her dream and became a national and international champion. She only recognized first place — everything that came below that wasn't good enough. Her bitterness set in as she realized that winning wasn't completely in her control, like when she couldn't compete because her ligaments were severely torn.

Or when her college boyfriend Tim, whom she planned to marry, cheated on her and left.

Using her determination, discipline and talents, she moved on and became a successful PR and marketing consultant. But she was too detached, and she didn't give herself enough time to process her grief and pain.

"[I got] really interested in things that just don't matter... climbing the corporate ladder, climbing the social ladder, living in a certain zip code in LA, having a certain view, having this, having that... It was about the having, not so much the being..."

She did a 'Tim search' every six months for 18 years. And she knows now that it wasn't really Tim she was looking for.

"I could never find him. The best way I can explain is it was just a spiritual longing... I was searching for Tim but I was really searching for God."

When they finally re-connected, Tim wanted to know what had happened to the real Dee, not the one who was hiding behind her social status and life that only looked good on the outside. I mention my favorite *Les Miserables* line: "To love another person is to see the face of God," and Dee explains:

"Yes. The human that God used in this case was Tim to bring me back to God. Subsequently the other reward was that I was brought back to Tim."

A beautiful cycle, and a process through which Dee healed and found her lost self.

"I just forgave him from the bottom of my heart, and then I forgave myself for not forgiving him. I had to forgive myself for harboring that bitterness, that anger and that pain for that long... That pain really steered the ship for a long time, and led me to making different choices that I otherwise would not have made had the pain not been there. I couldn't do it on my own strength. I couldn't forgive him on my own."

Reconnected to God, Dee healed from her pain and was also reconnected with the person she was always meant to be - the one who loves to help others, use her gifts to make this world a better place, and live as a true champion in life.

Dee Worley is known in the world of sports as Dee Foster, USA and

NCAA national and International Gymnastics champion. Today, Dee is a sought-after global branding, marketing, PR and business consulting expert who talks about how a long-lost love helped her to awaken to her purpose.

WATCH: When Love Brings an Awakening (with Dee Worley) (EP 22)
LISTEN: "Not Cool Enough" (by Tajci)

PONDER: Because humans are social beings, we understand Divine Love best through romantic relationships.

APPLY: Think of one person you love. How does that love make you feel? List all the feelings you feel. How many of those feelings describe how you feel about God? The deeper and more intimate our love is, the more feelings are going to match.

TWENTY-ONE

WHAT DO YOU DO WITH SMALL POCKETS OF TIME?

Time passing is a great trigger of awakening.

DURING SUMMER VACATIONS, my kids and I go through their school papers and pull out pieces that I'll keep, like writing assignments and impressive math tests. The real gems are random pieces of paper on which I find some of my kids' most creative work— doodles, cartoons and one-line reminders.

To me, it's an act of capturing the moments of their lives that aren't otherwise recorded, moments that happen on ordinary school days and go unnoticed by cameras and unmentioned on social media.

My mother kept a box of my earliest doodles, short poems, school work and idea plots, and whenever I go through it, something special happens. Even though these doodles don't necessarily trigger any specific memories, they help me remember the pockets of time that usually get lumped together in larger chapters marked by birthday pictures, recitals and graduations — pockets of time that shaped me when no one was paying much attention.

A few years ago, I found this doodle on my son's math worksheet. He was probably in 4th grade then. I loved the heels he drew on my feet, and I chuckled at the music above my head indicating my singing career. I tried really hard to keep myself from falling apart when I realized that my son had practiced multiplication on the number of times he called to me before I responded.

"Did I respond?" I asked myself silently.

GNOME ON THE ROAM COMES TO RESCUE

I met Anne Armstrong through an online business course we both took, and her *My Gnome on the Roam* project really spoke to me. At the time, I was looking for ways to better balance my new career path with my kids' growing needs to connect and have my attention, so that I wouldn't feel that exhausting "guilty" feeling of missing out and not doing "enough."

My Gnome on the Roam: a Glitter and Glue Covered Revolution is her unique solution to this challenge. Anne had always known she wanted to be of service to others, do something creative and be a mom. She accomplished the first two when she became a middle school teacher of gifted children. The mommy piece was a bit more complicated.

She met her husband as she was approaching 40 and although both of them were, as she says, "on board of the Baby train," her body wasn't. So they decided to adopt. The day they were matched with a family, their baby was born.

"It was magic. Talk about life turning on a dime... I'm forever in gratitude to the birth mother who gave us the opportunity..."

Anne had waited and yearned for this moment for a long time, so when it came, she soaked up every moment of it. And still, she noticed, the time was slipping away. Because it always does.

"I just very quickly felt like I blinked and he was walking. And I blinked again and his curls going away, and he was becoming a little man and so... I was rushing home at the end of the day and trying to squeeze dinner and laundry and time together..."

Her sister had five children at the time and Anne wondered, "How does anybody ever have quality time and maintain their sanity at the same time?"

WAKING UP TO THE STATISTIC AND DECIDING TO HELP PARENTS TO CHANGE IT

"I was just poking around and I found a statistic that said that the average family spends only less than 40 minutes per week of connected time."

Anne decided to combine her passions for teaching, creativity, and motherhood in an effort to change the situation, and channeled her energy into creating the *My Gnome on the Roam* project. It's a children's book, activity kit, video library and an app that offers feasible ways for parents and their kids to connect and engage.

"It's yet another thing that I can't fit into my schedule," I thought. But before I could verbalize how I felt, Anne explained how this project is different:

"We wanted to inspire families to just take little pockets of time that might otherwise be wasted. Fifteen minutes is enough to blow that statistic that we just talked about out of the water."

My Gnome on the Roam is designed to provide parents with the tools and inspiration to build creativity, a sense of adventure, and to forge deeper connections. On top of which, as Anne points out, kids will have long-term benefits from this connected time with improvements in their behavior, grades, self-esteem, health and well-being.

BEING PRESENT IN EVERY BLINKING MOMENT

For me, becoming aware of how to take advantage of these 'little pockets of time that might otherwise be wasted' is a revolutionary solution. I don't have to try to make extra time, or feel bad when I'm already overwhelmed. I can just focus on what I do have.

This fits into the concept that time is experienced differently when we are fully present. When we connect in the 'now,' time doesn't seem to rush into the future, as it seems to do when we are consumed with distractions that either keep us in the past or make us anticipate the next moment. And with children, it's easy to look at them, remember the days gone by and recognize that the day will soon come when they will be all grown up.

Not too long ago, at the end of a perfect and relaxing day, my teenage son came to me and sat on my lap. I held him the way I did when he was a little baby. I could feel my legs going numb under his weight.

"It seems like I blinked and you grew from a tiny little baby into a beautiful big boy," I said, kissing him on his forehead and squeezing him tightly in my arms.

"Don't blink, Mama," he said and smiled at me. We both held on to the moment.

"I'm going to blink and enjoy watching you grow between those blinks," I said. "With my eyes and my heart wide open, and my phone off."

And hopefully those pockets of time will never again be wasted or go unnoticed.

Anne Armstrong is a mother, middle school teacher and a published children's author from Nashville, Tennessee. Inspired by a statistic that revealed to her how little quality time parents spend with their children, Anne created and launched a project called My Gnome On The Roam, designed to help create stronger, happier kids, and more present and connected adults.

WATCH: Making Quality Family Time (with Anne Armstrong) (EP 23)
LISTEN: "Wynken, Blynken and Nod" (by Tajci)

PONDER: When we hit a certain age, or watch our kids grow 'too fast' we start paying more attention to time, and the shift to live with joy and purpose becomes urgent, because we don't want to 'waste another minute on unimportant stuff.'

APPLY: Think of a time that seemed to pass extremely fast. How much detail can you remember? Do an experiment and next time you are in a moment you want to remember bring yourself to the presence. Register small details around you. Be aware of your breathing and your feelings. Does it seem the time slows down when you do that?

TWENTY-TWO

WHEN ART SETS US FREE FROM FEELING INADEQUATE

Engaging in creative activity nourishes the soul.

"I WAS TIRED OF FEELING MYSELF INADEQUATE," Olga said to me in her charming Russian accent during our interview for *Waking Up in America*. There was no self-pity in her voice, only a matter-of-fact manner and a passion for life.

The two of us were sitting in her art gallery (named simply "O") talking about the waking up moment that shifted Olga's life and launched her into the world of art, entrepreneurship, and teaching.

We were surrounded by her eclectic paintings mounted on the walls from floor to ceiling. But it wasn't only canvases and prints that filled every inch of the beautiful space in Nashville's popular Marathon Village. The colors, the themes, styles and staging in her paintings exuded the story not so much of her life's events, but of her spirit - of risk, love, courage, freedom and confidence.

Olga Alexeeva was a Russian stage actress who came to America in 1991 to join her sister when the Berlin Wall fell and the big shift in Eastern European communist countries began to happen.

Life in America was radically different from anything Olga had known.

"The first ten years took me to speak English, because I came with no language. I remember the first time I saw a checkbook... I was a grown woman with a child, and I'd never seen a checkbook. I remember how... I was amazed by richness of Walmart. I hit my head through the door because it was so clean I didn't see it and boom... That was 'waking up in America'... And I remember that my first photo I sent to Russia, was from a grocery store."

Slowly, with the support and kindness of people she met in Nashville, her new life began to take shape "like from crumbles of the dough in a bowl."

But this physical shift of switching continents, of moving from one culture to a completely different one, was only a part of her path in truly stepping into the life she was meant for.

Russia had provided Olga with a free education; a college degree in acting led to a respectable job at a government-sponsored repertory theater. She learned and developed discipline, excellence, and a sense of striving for perfection, but there were also limitations that stifled her potential to be a creative artist, a powerful entrepreneur and an influential community leader.

America provided Olga with the support she needed to make another shift, a much more important internal one.

LISTENING TO THE SOUL'S HUNGER AND FINDING NEW PATHS

"When I came here, and I satisfied my hunger for food, for shelter, for everything, my soul was hungry for creativity."

Olga tried ballroom dancing and public speaking, and only considered a painting class so she could take it off her list of possibilities.

For years she held onto her insecurities, and her life seemed like a daily reminder of it.

"All children spoke English and I didn't. Think about it. Little baby, little child speaks English and I, an adult can not. That's already a shift, so that kind of added to my insecurity... I never considered paintings as one of my activities because I knew I could not paint."

Insecurity is one of those things we aren't born with. We learn it. We start believing that we are simply not good enough. Insecurity feeds into our sense of inadequacy and because of it, we often never even attempt to try what our hearts long for. "I can't sing. I can't dance. I can't paint. I can't believe in miracles. I can't heal. I can't surrender to love..." Most of us have said something along these lines at some point in our lives. Most of us accept those lines as our own - as if we have been given a script from which we say those lines and never doubt that perhaps, the script we are reading from is really someone else's, not our own.

And most of us need a prompt, a wake-up call, an angel, God-in-some-skin, to help us open our eyes and realize we CAN change the course of the story that IS our own.

"Hazel King, she is a legend in town... she welcomed me with the open arms and an open heart..."

It was King, a talented local painting instructor, who prompted Olga to let go of her insecurities. King believed in Olga when Olga didn't believe in herself. And that was enough to launch.

"I just started to go. I started to paint and step by step, I painted more and more and went to different classes and I started to do different shows. It was just like [when] you start skiing. Stand there!

Hey, go! And too-doot, I even could not stop!"

Olga owns two galleries and an art studio where she now teaches her own painting classes. She gives credit to the community that not only allowed her to thrive, but supported her every step of the way.

"I consider that not just my only personal achievement, but the Nashville itself... It's the biggest part of it."

I smile as I contemplate the journey Olga has taken. When we chose to seek deeper joy and purpose for our lives, teachers and guides appear to support us with exactly what we need — a prompt, a "borrowed belief" or a permission to be free and courageous. And when we step into the life we are created for, we become community influencers, we uplift others and accept with gratitude that we are a part of a bigger picture.

And speaking of pictures, what is your creative outlet you've been ignoring because you "feel yourself inadequate?" What would happen if you gave yourself permission to try anyway? Or if you felt completely free to make mistakes, fail and start over?

Perhaps Olga's story and her words can be your prompt:

"Also, [in America] I learned that I can make a mistake. I can make a mistake but then I can overcome it. Because life is so short and so precious."

Olga Alexeeva is an artist, entrepreneur and owner of the fine art 'O' Gallery located in Marathon Village, Nashville, Tennessee. She also teaches painting classes through which she inspires, empowers and helps students to overcome their fears and insecurities.

WATCH: Art, Russia and Waking Up in America (with Olga Alexeeva)

(EP24)

LISTEN: "Moscow Nights" (sung by Olga and Tajci)

PONDER: After she learned the language and was able to make a living, Olga looked for ways to nourish her soul and found art.

APPLY: Assuming that your basic physical needs are covered and you are safe, what are you doing for your soul? How do you fill your soul every day and let it grow and expand?

PART FOUR

*Be the change
you wish to see in the world.*
- Gandhi

TWENTY-THREE

HOW FORMER NFL RUNNING BACK TIM WORLEY FOUND HIS MOST IMPACTFUL GAME

*When we take on the identity of what we do, we feel safe.
But not for long.*

IT'S NOT EVERY DAY I GET TO MEET FOOTBALL STARS. As a matter of fact, I am one of "those people" who only watches the Super Bowl for the halftime show. I don't know much about American football, but I do enjoy experiencing and pondering its social impact. I often joke that, given its place in American culture, it really should be a part of the American citizenship test for us immigrants: "1. Name the current president of the USA, your state governor and your local mayor. 2. Who does Tom Brady play for? Who is Tim Tebow?"

So, when I interviewed Tim Worley for *Waking Up in America*, I really should have been more nervous. But I wasn't.

Tim was there with his wife Dee, whom I interviewed first. We spoke about her past as a former national and international gymnastics champion and also about the amazing love story she had to tell. She shared a side of Tim that was vulnerable, real, broken and restored. By the time I sat down with Tim, I was no longer interviewing the running back who was a first-round draft pick for the NFL and the superstar athlete who played for the Pittsburgh Steelers and the Chicago Bears. I was sitting down with an incredible human — a soul on a journey.

Tim was raised in a family of five boys, in a small North Carolina town. All of the boys played sports, and for Tim, the field was a place where he could release the frustration caused by his father's drinking and physical abuse of his mother. In high school, the world of sports was the place where he could feel good and secure about himself.

"I was the one that would never raise his hand, even if I knew the answer because I wasn't too sure about myself. But I was very sure about myself Friday night on a football field."

Tim thrived as an athlete, recognizing that he had a gift, but also working hard, because he "wanted to be better." He would train hard, running stadiums, hills, and around the campus with weights on his shoulders.

"If I felt tired or lazy, or didn't feel like it... That's the time that I pushed myself."

The sport became who he was.

It happens to many people who find their passion and their sense of self in what they do. For a long time I didn't know who I was outside of my music career, and ice skating champion Lucinda Ruh had a similar story that we explored in my episode "Finding Lucinda in the Queen of Spin."

Of course, this losing the sense of ourselves in the roles we play is not something that only happens to celebrities or champions. We may have jobs we are passionate about. We may try to create dream lives with perfect marriages and perfect parenthoods that lead us into an unhealthy imbalance where we lose connection with ourselves outside these roles. In addition, these outside successes validate us and offer external approval, that, as Tim says, feels good and helps to keep us stuck.

"I took on this identity [of a star athlete] because ... when I took that on, I felt good about myself. That was my sanctuary. When you come in this sanctuary you don't have to battle."

With his determination, discipline and natural gifts, Tim steadily rose to superstardom. He was an All-American running back for the University of Georgia, and was a first-round draft pick for the NFL as a running back. But too soon he got lost in a world which requires more than physical strength in order to thrive, not just as an athlete but as a whole person.

"I had no idea the course, the path that drugs and alcohol was going to set me on, even though it was very recreational and innocent...

When I got into the NFL and signed these huge contracts ... you didn't have to buy this stuff. It was there. It was given to you. You go to a party, you see marijuana, you see cocaine, you see pills, you see girls everywhere, all types of stuff, and so when you don't know who you are, how do you resist that? You go from, you know, having a couple of hundred of dollars in your account to ... now you got 3.5 million dollars in your bank account overnight. What do you do with that?"

I listen to Tim as he speaks about these experiences during his NFL career and I can't help but feel compassion and a sense of sadness. This is not just Tim's story; it's been repeated over and over in the media.

"When I got exactly what I wanted from the Steelers, what do I do? I went out and I sabotaged it. I went out and I got high, because deep down I was afraid of the opportunity and the responsibility that came with that."

Tim played 7 years in the NFL and when he retired from the Chicago Bears, he was lost.

"I started competing when I was 10, and all of a sudden I'm 30 years old and it's over. So what do you do when the cheering stops?"

It got ugly before it got better for Tim. Even though he was in therapy and recovery programs, he hit the bottom and after a publicly broadcast incident with a Smyrna, GA traffic officer, Tim ended up spending 23 days in jail.

"God answered my prayers. He saved my life. He put an angel in a cop's uniform to stop me in my tracks, to save my life that night."

While he was living out his sentence, Tim shifted into a sense of self that wasn't defined by his athletic successes and failures. With the same discipline and determination he had shown on the field, Tim stepped out onto a new path as a life skills consultant who is to this day changing the lives of young athletes and all who hear him speak or receive his one-on-one mentoring.

"There is more of an impact now on my life, on other people than my athletic career ... I know what it's like to be addicted to alcohol, I know what it's like to be addicted to drugs, I know what it's like to be addicted to a certain lifestyle, to women, to things that people tell us we are supposed to have, or what we are supposed to be like, or what's going to make us a man."

Recently, I found myself sitting in the bleachers at a high school football game. None of my three sons are involved in the sport, but we were there for the team spirit and the band.

Watching the young men on the field and my boys sitting next to me, I felt deep gratitude to Tim Worley. Perhaps people like Tim are meant to learn these important life lessons the hard way, to live these extreme lives so they can serve as teachers, guides and coaches.

Because when they say "yes" and awaken to their higher purpose, the impact they are able to make on our lives is huge. Beautiful and moving. Like an awesome touchdown. Do I dare say, more lasting?

Tim Worley is a former University of Georgia All-American and NFL running back who played for the Pittsburgh Steelers and the Chicago Bears. Today, Tim is a John C. Maxwell-certified leadership educator, life skills consultant and motivational speaker at Worley Global Enterprises.

WATCH: Waking up from a NFL Dream (with Tim Worley) (EP 25)
LISTEN: "I Will Stand" (by Scott Mulvahill)

PONDER: The insecurity that comes from not knowing who we really are may cause us to sabotage our career and success.

APPLY: Have you ever done something so successful and doubted you could ever repeat it? Have you pursued success and kept succeeding at the cost of growing spiritually or loosing a connection with someone you loved? Are you still caught up in either of those cycles? Bring your awareness to it and go back to the question: "Why am I doing what I'm doing." Be honest with yourself.

TWENTY-FOUR

FINDING HEALING IN 'PORTRAITS IN FAITH'

Listening to people talk about their journey is transformational.

"AT AGE 36 THE WORLD BROUGHT ME TO MY KNEES. And I prayed to a God I did not know." I paused the video on the *Portraits in Faith* website to take these words in. I recognized and identified with the feeling behind them.

The feeling of a desperate longing to be heard, accepted, healed... and to be found worthy of love. I pressed play again: "I realized I needed to be reminded of God's presence. So I picked up a camera."

It was May of 2013 when Sally, a friend from church, told me about Daniel Epstein's launch of *Portraits in Faith*, a series of video interviews and black-and-white portraits featuring people of all different faiths and cultures.

I spent hours reading and watching everything posted. While my kids and my husband were asleep I took advantage of the solitude and silence in which I was able to really listen to the interviews. I listened without judgment or fear, letting these people bless me and heal me despite our differences.

Like Daniel, I was in the process of healing, and the fact that he looked in many places for God and with such an open heart felt comforting to me.

At that particular time, I had hit a bump on my own spiritual path. I had gone from atheism to an awareness of God's presence in my life; from finding my faith home in the Catholic church to feeling confused when my soul longed to grow, expand and ask questions. I was scared of rejection and at the same time I wanted badly to listen to my soul, instead of worrying about 'doing or thinking something wrong.'

Daniel interviewed me for the *Portraits in Faith* series a few months later in September of 2013. I was nervous about telling my faith story, knowing full well that I was in a middle of another 'spiritual growth spurt.'

But the search for God is at the heart of Daniel's project, and growth is its ever-flowing pulse.

I thought of Daniel when I began to explore the waking up moments in people's lives on *Waking Up in America*. The moments when we summon our courage and search for purpose, meaning, and deeper connections in our lives — either without fear of judgment or rejection, or by facing the fear and inviting it to come along.

Daniel and I meet in Cincinnati at the home of a friend he often visits. He tells me how he was the guy with a good life, happy and successful in his career, but plagued by thoughts like, "I shouldn't have been born. I was a mistake. Nothing in life is fair. How much longer?" He tried to surround himself with other people in order to feel better, but that only resulted in too many broken relationships, which left him feeling even worse.

In our interview, Daniel brings up the neurosis caused by our unique human ability (courtesy of our pre-frontal cortex) to worry about the future and get depressed about the past. This neurosis can drive humans into all kinds of destructive behaviors and, as Daniel believes, can only be overcome by a spiritual journey.

So how does someone with a 'very analytical mind,' who as a marketing consultant works heavily with cognitive and behavioral sciences, get out of his head and connect with his spiritual self?

Daniel's journey began at a moment when he finally asked for help. It was his first 'authentic prayer,' he says. Then he started praying on his knees -- with a 'please' in the morning and a 'thank you' at night. Having grown up Jewish in the South, he had participated in many interfaith events and had always 'believed in many paths.' So, he didn't limit the guidance he sought to the Jewish faith alone.

A hand analysis given by a friend interested in palmistry triggered in Daniel an awareness of the need to heal.

"...the teacher said, Oh, you want to heal. And I said heal myself or others? And she said you want to heal. You want to reclaim every part of yourself and in so doing you won't be able to help but heal others."

Portraits in Faith started as a project for a summer photography workshop. Daniel's global job with a big company at the time provided an opportunity to travel the world, and he would hire producers in different cities and line up 4-5 people a day to interview them and make a portrait: "I figured if I could just hear people talk about their divine journey, their transformations, that I could draft off of those and it would somehow heal me."

The portraits were healing. Not only for Daniel, but as the teacher said, his process allowed for others to be healed as well. He filmed over 400 interviews in 27 different countries and representing over 50 religions. Daniel thought of putting it all together into a film, but he didn't like the idea of having to cut so many people out of the story. When the award-winning documentary filmmaker Ken Burns said to him, "Have the courage to say this isn't a film," Daniel decided a digital approach was the only way to honor each person. He started a website to which one person's portrait is added every week.

The interviews are shot with a single camera and minimally produced, which gives *Portraits in Faith* a raw, intimate and authentic encounter with people you wouldn't necessarily encounter at your Sunday service. But each of them offers the opportunity to expand your mind and connect with your soul.

"... if you choose the spiritual approach to life then every part of life is on the spiritual journey, even when we aren't where we ultimately want it to be. Even the person who I might judge who is doing behaviors X, Y and Z... And I have to remember to bless everyone on their journey and... honor their journey and know that they are exactly where they're supposed to be."

And that for me is why I spent hours exploring *Portraits in Faith* that first night and again since then, and why I am grateful to Daniel for bringing this project to us.

I find it to be a place where we can all meet each other and feel heard, accepted and healed. Where we can honor each other's journey, recognizing our common pain and our shared longing for Love without judgment or fear.

Daniel Epstein is a marketing and innovation consultant based in Toronto, Canada, who, in search to fill the God-sized hole in his life created Portraits In Faith, *a global project documenting the role of spiritual experience inside and outside of formal religion, expected and unexpected, told in people's own words, and brought to life with video and photography.*

WATCH: Waking up with Desire to Fill the God-sized Hole (with Daniel Epstein) (EP 26)

LISTEN: Eli atah v'odeka, elohai aromemeka. (From Hallel, Psalm 118) (sung by Daniel Epstein)

PONDER: When we share our experiences with each other, when we listen to the stories of fellow travelers, we learn about ourselves and it helps us to transform our lives.

APPLY: Find a story of someone who is of a very different spiritual or religious background from you. Or talk to someone like that in person. Listen to them without reacting or making judgements. Let your heart be open. How do you feel afterwards? What do your feelings tell you about where you are on your spiritual journey?

TWENTY-FIVE

HOW VOLUNTEERING CAN HELP THE WORLD (AND YOU)

Create that which you need to lift you up. The process will make it happen.

THERE ARE SOME DAYS WHEN YOU READ THE NEWS and, no matter how sincerely you send out your prayers, think positive thoughts, and focus on all that you are grateful for, you still feel pain for those who are suffering. You are desperate to do more, but in the big scope of things you feel helpless. And then from the shadows comes self-doubt, saying: "You can't do anything about it."

If you are operating under less than optimal conditions (exhaustion from trying to make ends meet, tending to your children, or taking care of your aging parents), you will likely lean into this feeling of helplessness and trigger a chain of fears that you are not doing enough, you are not being enough, or that you don't deserve the life you have. If you let that fear take over, you become unable to function at all -- let alone help the world.

Or if you don't get fearful, perhaps you get angry at those who are to blame for all the pain, and the anger takes you down a rabbit hole of darker and darker thoughts.

Sure, you can numb your pain, anger and fear, but that will keep you stuck in a vicious cycle and further prevent you from really showing up and "doing something about it."

That's one cycle.

Then there is this one: You send out your prayers, think positive thoughts, focus on all that you are grateful for, AND you still feel pain for those who are suffering. You embrace it, because you know that we are all part of one human family and that it's normal to feel each other's pain. You know that you feel the pain of every suffering soul because you care and love. And when doubt, fear and anger surface, you don't get stuck — you lean into the love a little bit more.

You choose to become even more aware of how each of us plays a very significant part. So you go about your day as usual, but you smile more intentionally, hold someone's hand a bit longer, and make choices that are a part of the solution, not the problem. You look for things to do that will truly make a difference.

Where these two cycles meet is volunteering.

There is nothing more healing for someone struggling with fear or lack of self-worth than helping others. And if it's true that the mile-long journey starts with a single step, then helping the world can start with doing something good right now, even if it seems inconsequential.

DOING GOOD IS NOT HARD

I met Megan McInnis, founder of Doing Good, a brand new 501c3 non-profit organization based in Nashville, Tennessee at the 2015 Nashville Film-Com event. I was drawn to her booth by the giant thumbs-up logo supporting the message of Doing Good.

Telling stories of people who are doing good in the world is my cup of tea, and I firmly believe that there can never be too much uplifting and inspirational content in the media. I love stories of real people doing awesome things, especially awesome things that everyone can do, but that we all forget to talk about because they always get overshadowed by big heroic stories which we love, but usually can't duplicate.

Megan's idea behind the television show also named Doing Good is to provide a platform featuring everyday volunteers and their stories, also serving as a resource and encouragement for anyone who doesn't know where to start or who finds themselves feeling that they aren't doing 'enough.'

The idea came out of her own need to be picked up when she had been laid off, recently divorced and was looking for something uplifting to watch on TV. She found nothing. Instead of despairing, Megan stepped into action and researched available domain names, and that's where she found *DoingGood.TV*.

She moved to Nashville and in the next two years sat down one-on-one with several hundred people, asking them questions about what worked and what didn't work, what they liked and didn't like about volunteering. She listened, she built a team of volunteers, and today her organization offers an extensive database of volunteering resources - for anyone who wants to volunteer, wants to find out more about volunteering or simply doesn't know where to start. She's also developing a TV show.

Megan comes from the world of marketing and PR. She worked for Disney as well as three of the largest non-profit organizations in the country, and along the way she realized that she wanted to focus on the people rather than the organizations themselves.

"We do believe that it's important to know who you are volunteering with and which organizations do what in your local communities, but in all honesty, every community has to deal with hunger and homelessness, and literacy, and more. And so I think that when we come together as a community and we talk about the cause, then frankly we can encourage people to do more."

During our conversation Megan mentions the value of practicing mindfulness in our volunteering. It's easy to feel we are not doing enough because we might not be doing the 'usual' volunteering jobs, like feeding the hungry, building houses or going on mission trips. I, for example, don't think of singing at my church or setting up stage lights for school events as volunteering.

"It's important to recognize those people who might not realize that they are volunteering... it's so easy to forget and not think about or not give yourself credit for [it]. We want to highlight people... who are out there making a difference in their own way."

The beauty of it all is an awareness of how our actions serve our world. Because we are all connected as one family, there is no such thing as one volunteering position being 'more important' than another. We all work together, using our unique gifts. And when we show up to help intentionally because we care and love, we do make a difference.

Megan McInnis president and executive director of Doing Good, a 501c3 non-profit organization that produces a TV show featuring volunteers who make a difference in other people's lives throughout the world, and who flourish in the enjoyment that comes from giving.

WATCH: Waking Up to Doing Good (with Megan McInnis) (EP 27)

LISTEN: "Fly" (by Debbie Cunningham)

PONDER: When Megan was down, she needed something to lift up her spirits. Stories of people Doing Good. The action of filling that need helped her awakening.

APPLY: What is it that you are missing most in your life right now? What can you do about it? There is always something you can do. Take a breath and take action. No matter how small it is. Move. Act. Right now.

TWENTY-SIX
HOW THIS ONE POET IS GIVING A VOICE TO THE VOICELESS

Practice being comfortable speaking your truth.

"PUT YOUR TWOS UP, KEEP THEM IN THE SKY / that's hand sign for peace / we all gotta try make a better way 'cause just the other day / I found out Eric Garner man he passed away..."

I stand behind the cameras and watch as Rashad thaPoet performs his poem "Put Ya 2s Up." He is deeply engaged, fully present and 'plugged in' to that undeniable life force that connects us all.

On Rashad's web site he calls it "spitting the truth," and I can see now what he means. It's a nonapologetic, confident and yet deeply vulnerable way of saying, "Hear me out. I've got something to say." We've just wrapped the interview for *Waking Up In America* in which I asked Rashad about the turning point in his life that put him on the path of becoming a poet, a spoken word artist and an educator who now helps thousands of youth to find their voice through poetry.

I feel the passion behind the carefully crafted words he sends out into the world. I feel the words transforming me — my eardrums turn the sound waves of each word into impulses that are translated by my brain, and the experience and the feeling behind the words — both mine and Rashad's — are sent out into the part of my body where my heart is. I can feel movement there, and I recognize it as my soul resonating with the honesty and hard truth of Rashad's poem.

> "... head down I send a prayer up
> his family looking around like who gonna take care of us
> hard to maintain with your head underwater
> chicken necks systems, can't get a grasp
> gaspin' for air when all they did was laugh
> Bilderberg Group Trilateral Commission
> Wizards of Oz no curtain needed
> they hide in plain site most just don't see it
> too busy in a struggle tryin' to make a livin'..."

Rashad was close to being caught in that life of being "too busy in a struggle tryin' to make a livin." From our conversation, I know that as a young father of two children there is a certain, unavoidable pressure of having to provide for and take care of his family.

He had originally set out to study mechanical engineering in order to secure a good job. But when he attended an open mike event at his college, Rashad sensed there was a part of him that he needed to find the courage to explore. He wasn't sure if he, too, could write and perform poetry, but he allowed the inspiration to work inside of him until he was ready.

After his very first performance at the same open mike event, he walked off with applause thundering in his ears and let out a big whoop. Did he feel liberation? Freedom? Joy? Courage in action? A newfound superpower? I wonder as I listen to him continue:

> "... now pass it on is the key

give back what you were given
zombies walk around but they're not really livin'..."

I smile from within. Not only does Rashad give back through his gift, but he is also truly passing it on to others. Yes, he is a recognized artist in Nashville and beyond, having released 14 CDs and received numerous awards and recognitions, but he is out there day by day teaching kids to express themselves through poetry and the spoken word.

We talk about his experience working with kids. "A lot of times they're forced to keep things inside and digest a lot of their feelings," Rashad points out. "If you shake up a Coke and then you open the top, it'll explode." I think how true this is in our society of "Facebook perfect" pictures, Instagram filters and the mentality of "keeping it all together." No wonder more and more kids are exploding these days. No wonder we are all falling apart.

"... folks all over been dealing with these capers
been over some years time some get to see paper
just tryin' a great escape
what's the point in the hate
we need to bounce back starts with the rap
is revolution time a resolute to climb
I'm trying to get higher..."

"What's the point in the hate," he says. And I realize he isn't just saying it... These words are coming from a deep place within his soul. Like music, it carries more than consonants and vowels. Again, my soul trembles as it adjusts to vibrate on Rashad's "higher" frequency.

I imagine thousands of young lives, and how uplifted and empowered they must feel when they hear Rashad perform in their schools, and when he teaches them how to express themselves and connect with others in the same vulnerable, real and courageous way — all within a few stanzas of spoken word.

> "... people listen close
> no man knows the hour so only fools boast
> they drag on squares then they let their mind coast
> drag on squares then they let their mind coast, ah
> songs of liberation they say give us free
> it's all about patience they just want peace
> Y'all put your Twos Up
> and never let them down
> Y'all put your Twos Up and never let them down."

For a moment no one says a word. The crew, me, our host at "O" Gallery... I want to thank Rashad with more than just words so I open my arms and reach in for a hug. It feels so good to have been blessed by Rashad (there really isn't a better word than "blessed"). I put my Twos Up in support of his music, his poetry, his mission and our common desire to make good, healing ripples of change in our world.

Rashad "thaPoet" Rayford is an activist, actor and an award-winning Spoken Word Artist from Nashville, Tennessee. He is a writer mentor at Southern Word, a nonprofit that seeks to empower the community's youth through the written and spoken word.

WATCH: Truth-Telling Through Spoken Word (with Rashad thaPoet) (EP 28)

LISTEN: "Put Ya 2's Up" (By Rashad thaPoet)

PONDER: It feels incredibly liberating to be able to speak your truth and feel you are being heard.

APPLY: What does 'speaking my truth' mean to you? Is it as simple as trying to tell someone how you feel and them not being able to understand, acknowledge or even hear you?

TWENTY-SEVEN

WHAT THIS STREET FIGHTER TURNED WORLD CHAMPION TAUGHT ME

Are you fighting from the place of fear and anger, or living from the place of love and compassion?

PHYSICAL FIGHTS ARE ONE THING I've always had a hard time understanding. I come from a non-violent musical family. The few fist fights I witnessed growing up came from either anger, exploding emotions, or alcohol, so it was always clearly a side-effect of a deeper problem. I also never got a chance to appreciate fighting as a sport. My only connection to Martial Arts was the movie *Karate Kid*.

I have three sons, and despite my desire to bring them up without fighting games or toy weapons, they always loved to wrestle, rough-house and find sticks that look like guns and pretend to be warriors.

Eventually, I gave up trying to prevent them from channeling their inner 'fighters' and even took them to laser tag and nerf war games.

Recently, a friend invited my 10- and 13-year-old sons to the "awesomest" nerf war in the area, at local gym and martial arts center MPact Sports in Franklin, Tennessee. My sweet boys came back raving about the fun they had.

"The best thing of all?" I asked. "Mr. Eric!" they unanimously agreed. "He is in charge of the whole thing, and he dresses up and he sets up the teams, and he is just awesome," said my 10-year-old with an excitement that made me question my decision to encourage the "war" game, since I really would prefer them to let out their energy by dancing or kicking a soccer ball.

But I had promised myself when my firstborn was still in my womb that I would not try to shape them into the people I wanted them to be, but only gently guide them into the people they were created to be.

"Mr. Eric was a world champion and he has a black belt," my 13-year-old reported. "I think he has a good story."

A STREET FIGHTER, WORLD CHAMPION AND TEACHER

A few weeks later, we're setting up our cameras on the floor of MPact sports to interview Eric for *Waking Up In America*. Eric's wife and CEO of the gym, DeeAnn, brings me a white dobak to wear. I look at my DP and he shrugs his shoulders as if to say this wasn't his idea.

But when I change into it and look at myself in the mirror some sleeping tiger inside of me wakes up, and for a moment I feel a desire to leap, kick and be unafraid of getting hurt. I ask Eric to show me some moves and take me down. He is careful and the floor is soft, so I giggle and enjoy myself, but then put the tiger back to sleep.

"Since my name is Tajci (and it sounds like Tai Chi, the martial art) I am taking Tai Chi," I tell Eric with a bit of pride. "I had too much aggression for Tai Chi," Eric says matter-of-factly, not hiding it. "Couldn't do it."

Eric is a fighter. He started out as a street fighter, hanging out with the kids on the "wrong side of the tracks" — robbing houses and cars, stealing and fighting. His mother fell ill when Eric was 11 or 12 and died several years later. His father "wasn't interested in family" and offered very little guidance to Eric, who says he was left to justify his actions on his own.

When he tells me how they would "get arrested from time to time," I actually had to interrupt him and bring the reality of it into my understanding. I want to cry for this child who was out there getting deeper and deeper into trouble without guidance or love that he could recognize.

During one arrest, a police officer presented him with a choice -- jail or martial arts.

It took Eric some time to learn how to train in class and build the discipline that all great fighters posses.

After many years of serving as a "feeder fighter" at a gym in Nashville, Eric got a chance to fight himself and even won a world championship. In the winning moment, looking at his capitulating opponent, Eric experienced a turning point that shifted him into a new life and helped him to see that Love had always been there.

Eric's story is one of forgiveness and overcoming the tremendous amount of obstacles on the path that eventually led him to carry the torch at the 1996 Olympic Games in Atlanta.

As a loving husband and father, a man filled with faith and an awareness of God "moving his life along," Eric eventually became a mentor and teacher, and he now offers guidance to kids by helping them to build their self-esteem and learn self-defense. His experience allows him to have a profound impact on young lives.

As we wrap up the interview, Eric tells me a story of a kid whom he helped shift from being a bully into becoming a balanced and successful person. I sense his gratitude for having this chance to pay forward what he received from the police officer who, years back, played the same part in his life: not discarding him as a "troublemaker," but seeing his potential and natural gift for being a fighter.

Before I leave, I hand my dobak to DeeAnn (whose performance of "Wayfaring Stranger" in our episode moves me to tears). I ask her if Eric teaches "family" classes that I could attend with my boys. I would love to learn and understand more about the fighting side of our human nature. Perhaps I'd even consider awakening the sleeping tiger inside me. She smiles at me and says: "Of course! And I'm sure you would love it."

Eric Melton is the owner and head of martial arts at MPact Sports in Franklin, Tennessee. A former Kickboxing Champion and a black belt, Eric works with children and youth to inspire them to develop their physical but also spiritual abilities.

WATCH: Fighting His Way Home (with Kickboxing Champion Eric Melton) (EP 29)

LISTEN: "Wayfaring Stranger" (sung by DeeAnn Melton)

PONDER: Master fighters fight from the place of love - to protect the innocent from the attackers. When we give into fear, anger and aggression, we lose.

APPLY: Take a Martial Arts class. Most of the rec centers and gyms have a free demo. Observe how it makes you feel.

TWENTY-EIGHT

HOW A LITTLE JAR OF BODY BUTTER FROM THISTLE FARMS HEALS EVERY BODY

Love heals every body.

I SCOOP UP A LITTLE DOLLOP OF BODY BUTTER from a small Thistle Farms jar and spread it on my legs. My skin looks tired and thirsty. "I haven't been gentle with myself lately," I think as I rub in the rich cream and take a deep breath. The sweet fragrance brings up this love-hate relationship I've had with my body ever since my teenage years, when I became aware that a woman's body can be mistaken for a commodity, something that can be used, demanded, bought, sold, or manipulated...

I reach for another scoop, and my eyes focus on the picture of the thistle flower on the jar. I'm momentarily transported from my bathroom to the place where this little jar comes from as I visualize the hands that mixed the ingredients, filled the jar, closed the lid and packed it with a card that says "Love Heals."

The hands that prepared this jar were the hands of women at Thistle Farms, a community of women who have survived prostitution, trafficking and addiction.

I don't know these women. I can't possibly imagine what they have gone through in their lives, but I feel close to them. I'm aware of the immensity of the kind of pain they've pushed through. I rub more body butter onto my arms and legs, letting the healing spread deeper than my skin. Gratitude washes over me.

I close my eyes and send a prayer of healing back to them and into the universe, to which we all belong as part of the same beautiful and broken body which can only be healed by love.

BECCA STEVENS - THE WOMAN BEHIND THE LITTLE JARS OF HEALING STUFF

I don't believe it's possible to have a lunch at the Thistle Farms' Cafe in downtown Nashville, use any of the "Love Heals" products, or read any of Becca's books without feeling surrounded by love, grace and healing. By the time I sit down with Becca for our interview on *Waking Up in America,* I've already begun to experience the incredible changes she and this powerful community of women are triggering in the world.

Becca Stevens is an Episcopal priest, social entrepreneur, author of nine books and founder of Thistle Farms. She was designated a White House Champion in 2011, and in 2013 was inducted into the Tennessee Women's Hall of Fame.

And under all the labels and achievements, she is a healer. She's an incredibly strong and confident woman, and at the same time a humble and vulnerable soul. Between segments of difficult topics we discuss, she makes us laugh with unpretentious and unguarded humor. She puts no walls up, has no masks on — it's just her and the truth 'as she understands it.' Her passion to heal women — and consequently the world — is contagious.

I want to know about how she overcame the sexual abuse she went through as a young, young girl. I want to know why she became a priest, especially after a church elder sexually abused her. How did she not get angry with God and run away?

"God was never my problem," she says.

Becca has a huge capacity for forgiveness, which is crucial in the healing process. "Mercy is a two-way street," she says matter-of-factly. This resonates with me. I think it's the only piece of wisdom anyone will ever need in order to let go of pain, fear and anger, even though the process is always going to be difficult.

And that's why she brings to focus the importance of community.

The same church community where her abuser served also helped her to heal (through acts of love and compassion both large and small.) I'm beginning to see why Becca is able to see beauty even in the ugliest corners of our society, where abuse, addiction, manipulation and greed have a grip.

Becca founded the organization under the name Magdalene first, to help women get off the street. Her toddler son noticed an advertisement for a strip joint called "The Classic Cat" in downtown Nashville and wanted to know why the lady in a catsuit was smiling.

"The question from my son just broke my heart. It was like, at some point he's not going to ask that anymore. This is gonna fade into the landscape of what we think is normal for women. And I didn't want him to think that I thought that was all right to buy and sell women for probably less than what you need to get a cat."

When she tells me why she named the residences after Mary Magdalene, I am left speechless, feeling the impact of the love she talks about:

"I always wanted to name it Magdalene... She was the first preacher. The reason the disciples got to hear the good news of how love heals is because of her and so whatever she went through in her life.... she's the common denominator at the tomb and it was as if Jesus was lingering for her to wait. That's how much she needed to know... I wanted to feel like love would linger for me and say it's going to take you a little bit and you have a lot of rough edges and we will stay long enough for you to hear it."

Today, the community that Becca started in 1997 is reaching women across the world through 18 global partners (including Rwanda and Ecuador) and 22 sister communities in the U.S. The women of Thistle Farms are given a chance to heal, restore their dignity and learn to thrive and flourish in a safe and supportive community. Over 80% of them succeed — much like the thistle that is known for its persistence in pushing through the dry, hard ground to grow, produce a beautiful purple flower and bring its healing properties into our world.

For me, the healing that I find in every jar of Thistle Farms' body butter comes with a chance to pause and consider how I treat my body, how I treat others in my community, and how I teach my three sons about the true meaning of love that 'lingers' and waits. It comes with a calling to keep working on my own heart and forgive, so I too can live out Becca's words: "I want to be as healthy as I can for my community."

Becca Stevens is an author, Episcopal priest, and the founder and president of Thistle Farms. She was named one of "15 Champions of Change" for violence against women in 2011 by the White House, Humanitarian of the Year in 2014 by the Small Business Council of America and the TJ Martell Foundation, and was inducted into the Tennessee Women's Hall of Fame in 2013. Her latest book, "Letters from the Farm: A Simple Path for a Deeper Spiritual Life," is available on Amazon.com.

WATCH: Love Heals Every Body (with Becca Stevens) (EP 30)
LISTEN: "I'm a Thistle Farmer" (by Dorris Walker)

PONDER: No matter how deep the wounds are that keep us feeling inadequate and unworthy of wholeness, healing IS possible through love and support of a community that believes in the healing power of love.

APPLY: Is there someone in your life who needs emotional healing? Reach out to them with love. Listen and let them know you are present to them. Don't be shy to tell them you love them and that they are indeed worthy of love.

TWENTY-NINE

LOVE THE HOMELESS - LESSONS FROM SANDY GRIFFIN

Homeless is not only a person who sleeps under a bridge.

COLLIN WAS WAITING FOR A LONG TIME for a chance to perform a song for us when we finished shooting *Waking Up in America*. He didn't have to be anywhere. No one was waiting for him. I had no idea that he was homeless.

He used to be a graphic designer who worked for a corporation with big ad accounts. Something broke in him, or awakened, when his son asked him what his job was. Collin heard himself answering: "I'm making people buy useless stuff they don't need." He quit his job, sold everything and spent time with his kid.

Somehow, he ended up on the streets of Nashville. His son is in college now, and Collin's eyes become alive with excitement when he talks about him.

Meeting Collin left me with many questions. Aren't we all more or less caught up in a system that "sells stuff we don't need" only to miss out on living? Is the only answer to Collin's homelessness to bring him back into the mindless rotation? Apart from each of us personally awakening to this truth, how can we fix this mess we are in?

SANDY GRIFFIN

I've heard a lot about Sandy Griffin, a professional speaker, life coach, author and a tireless advocate for the homeless. I knew she was out there on the front lines daily, and I wanted to talk to her.

We met at a Radiant Health Institute workshop. Long after the talk she gave was over, her message stuck with me: "Find out who you are first before you go out to serve the world."

Sandy has been dubbed "Life's Cheerleader," but like all people who bring us joy, she understands suffering and is not afraid to show pain. If you hang around her long enough, she will pull two red noses out of her purse and hand you one, saying, "You have to be able to laugh at yourself." And you will be compelled to put one on your nose immediately.

She grew up in a family of 12 kids. She was a compulsive overeater for 30 years, and she's survived cancer three times. When her marriage of 20 years ended in a divorce, she felt completely lost.

Here is what I learned from Sandy over the course of filming our episode *Waking Up and Loving the Homeless*.

1. Losing ourselves is like losing everything. Without knowing who we are, we are disconnected and displaced. Our soul feels the absence of a home.

After her divorce, Sandy volunteered in Haiti after the earthquake and in Waveland, Mississippi after the hurricane hoping to find comfort in serving others.

"... I remember standing there with all these people thinking I'm finding out who I am just like they are. I felt like I lost everything, they lost all their physical stuff. I lost myself and right then I went, I'm home!"

This perspective on what it really means to "be home" is the key to changing how we see the homeless. It allows us to realize that we are not very different from each other. In our core, we share the same longing — of finding a place to belong.

2. We must shed the lies we allowed ourselves to believe in order to be who we are.

Broken with insecurities, Sandy was repeatedly told that she wasn't smart enough, didn't sound educated enough and couldn't do anything. She believed the lies. At Waveland, her job was to stand in front of the receiving tent and talk to people, and it was here she became aware of her gifts for connecting with people and encouraging them. This experience eventually led her to become a confident thought leader and influencer.

"... all of a sudden I realized standing there, this is who I am! I have a great sense of humor, I can love on these people, I can give to them, I can pray with them and all of a sudden it all came together..."

How do we become aware of the lies we are buying into? How do we discern what is good and what is abusive in our system? And how do we make a change? What went wrong in Collin's life when he refused to work all the time so he could influence people to buy "useless stuff they didn't need"? But imagine how much can go right when we live from our truth and become game-changers and create new, better systems of socially conscious enterprise.

3. Practicing self-care is not selfish, it's restorative. You can't

help anyone if you are exhausted or unhealthy. But don't hide your pain either.

Sandy's eating disorder started when her dad got sick and her mother was unable to provide emotional support to the children. "It was a way of taking care of ourselves," Sandy says about how she and her sister would spend all of their profits from delivering newspapers on candy. Her addiction lasted thirty years.

"Awareness is everything," she coaches. Take time to rest, to pray, meditate, walk. Know when you are running on limited resources and are starting to disconnect. When you are not facing the cause of your anxiety or worry, it's more likely that you will reach for an 'easy button,' like food, excessive shopping, or drugs.

"... when you are out in the world doing what's not you, you are wearing a coat that doesn't fit; you make it fit, but it's not comfortable..."

Our mindless running around is precisely what feeds the system of 'useless stuff we don't need.'

And that's how we only perpetuate the problem. So, the answer IS in personal awakenings, and in developing an awareness as to what it means to live your life, rather than just make your way through it.

"... when you're saying ... I have to work, I have to get my kids' homework, I have to take them to this, what you're saying to your kids is, this is what your life is going to be like ... the stuff of the world is more important than you and I sitting here eye to eye..."

Collin stayed around because he didn't have anywhere else to go. He was so present in the moment, I felt jealous. He wasn't anxious to leave, or restlessly searching for his phone to check his messages. He connected with us, and for a while we all felt at home with each other sharing stories, music and just being ourselves.

That's exactly what Sandy does when she works with the homeless. It's how she is changing lives everywhere, as she shows the rest of us how to love the homeless (and each other).

Sandy Griffin is a professional speaker, coach, author and a tireless advocate for the homeless. Find Sandy on Facebook to get involved with loving the homeless. She is the proud mother of three beautiful daughters, Jacki, Katie and Lauren.

WATCH: Waking Up and Loving the Homeless (with Sandy Griffin) (EP 31)

LISTEN: "When I Leave This Town" (by The Trespassers)

PONDER: Home is a sense of belonging, connection. Sandy identified with the homeless after she lost a sense of who she was.

APPLY: Where is your home? What does 'being at home' look like? How does if feel? Write down those feelings. How many of those words describe the feeling of 'belonging'? What can you do to help the homeless?

THIRTY

PEACE WITHOUT UNDERSTANDING

Thoughts and feelings are also a part of self-care.

I SIT DOWN AT MY FAVORITE COFFEE SHOP to write this story. I take in the beauty and the blessing of another gorgeous day and exhale in gratitude. Next to me in a brown paper box are three delicious homemade muffins loaded with chocolate chips that I've bought for my sons. I imagine their eyes smiling when they get them, and the thought fills me with instant joy.

The story I'm writing is about the tremendous impact one woman has made on me. I met her at a holistic retreat, and subsequently interviewed her for *Waking Up in America*.

Robin Mizaur is a former Marine, holistic life coach, personal trainer and a certified nutrition consultant. She also works with The Heimerdinger Foundation delivering organic food to cancer patients.

I pause and feel a pang of guilt. I shouldn't have bought those muffins.

Robin brought a green drink to the retreat to share with participants and talked about healthy habits. When we filmed our episode, she came in with two jars of freshly squeezed green juice with "Packed with Love" lids. "Afternoon refreshment," she said. "It will renew your energy and your cells will thank you."

Robin is a petite woman. The Marines had to custom-make her boots; in kids' sizing she wears a 2. "They gave me one pair of boots and they said, they better last you your whole enlistment," she laughed.

My first thought was, sure, it's easy for her to switch from chocolate chip muffins to green juice smoothies! It takes tenacity and discipline just like what you need to complete Marine Corps training.

But Robin doesn't use scare tactics. She is gentle and reassuring.

"There is always something that you can start doing this moment... Whether it's increasing your water intake, whether it's taking three minutes to take three deep breaths and breathe the way we are supposed to breathe. Those are successes..."

It's the deep understanding, love and compassion she radiates with that draws me in. It quiets the old refrain in my head: "It's too hard. I could never do it," and turns up the volume of something different.

"When I [coach] people... I notice that there is lack of love for themselves. Loving yourself makes you a better mom, a better wife, a better companion, a better partner, a better employee... It's not something selfish, because if you are loving yourself you can give more love to others."

I pause and take a sip of the water I ordered for myself with those muffins. I breathe in a deep breath and a surge of tears tickles my nose and blurs my vision.

"Why is that so hard to do?" I asked Robin during our conversation. Is becoming aware of what we feed our bodies, how we nourish them, a good place to start? Treating ourselves like we would treat our children, taking care of them, keeping them healthy? (The muffins in the box start looking more and more like little monsters.)

Robin points out how important it is to be aware of everything that feeds not just our bodies, but also our heart, our mind and our soul.

"... More than nutrition are words and thoughts and feelings... 'cause each one of those have a chemical reaction, hormonal reaction in our body."

PEACE WITHOUT UNDERSTANDING

Robin lost her son in a tragic accident when he was 23 years old. They had a close, loving relationship. "What did you do?" I asked, imagining pain so deep it's paralyzing.

"Lots of crying... my fiancé at the time, now my husband, took me to a counselor... all I remember is she said, don't get stuck in the 'what ifs'... 'what if this, what if that...' I just took that little bit of information with me and it took me days to process. And through it, it's been four years now, I have learned to turn those 'what ifs' to 'what would.' Like, what would Anthony be doing, what would he love to see me doing."

She didn't push the pain away, didn't try to numb it and that helped her to not get stuck in it. Right away she became aware that if she was ever going to heal, she had to turn to love. Family and friends surrounded her with support and she accepted it.

This action of accepting the love that was there for her healed, little by little, the pain of being physically removed from the love that was taken away in the tragedy.

"I just prayed... and asked for peace without understanding... I wake up every day with a broken heart, but I take that pain that I feel and just turn it into love. That is like the most important thing and when no matter where you're at in your life, love is just... it's so important..."

Robin takes each thought, each feeling, each experience of love, healing and peace without understanding and shares them with others. She does the same with her green juice, and she labels it all with the words "Packed with Love." That's what she teaches wholeheartedly as a nutrition consultant and holistic life coach: that making changes in our lives starts with choosing love. Always. Choosing. Love.

I pick up the muffins and rush home. I can't wait to hug my boys. And I realize, the tiny moment of seeing the joy in their eyes when I give them the chocolate chip-loaded muffins is really just an instant gratification... mostly for me. And that on occasion, it's okay. It's life's little pleasures that we will remember when we grow old.

But what stays forever is love. Love, which reminds me to right now not feel shame or guilt for getting those deliciously made muffins, (because the person who made those muffins 'packed them with love' too) but to take little steps. Like stopping at the store and picking up some organic lettuce and making a big salad to eat first.

Robin Mizaur is a former United States Marine, a certified Personal Trainer, Nutritional Consultant and a Holistic Life Coach specializing in Wellness. Robin is one of the founders of Happy Nash, a community dedicated to teach and deliver a daily dose of healthy lifestyle habits.

WATCH: Love and Healing After Tragedy (with Robin Mizaur) (EP 32)

LISTEN: "I Pray" (by Tajci)

PONDER: When we are not well, we aren't able to transform our lives. Like in nature, we stay dormant until it's safe to proceed. Through self-care and support of family and friends we heal.

APPLY: Are you gentle with yourself? Or tough? There are times for both. Assess your well being — physical, psychological and emotional and then proceed. And ask for others to support you when you need it.

THIRTY-ONE

WAKING UP TO DANCE, MINDFULLY

Tears are like a river. They get you to where you have to be to heal.

THE SONG STARTS AND I LET MY BODY RESPOND. My hips sway and my feet start to step this way and that. My arms lift up above my bobbing head and my hands shake as if clearing the air off. As I breathe faster and shallower, my body responds to the music wanting to move even more, fast, and free. I feel my temperature rising and my heart racing, and a giggle forms in my chest. Laughter, joy, abandonment fill me.

"Oh, I forgot how good this feels," I think, and let that thought pass without judgment. All that matters is that it feels good right now. I'm not getting stuck on beating myself up for forgetting to dance, or not having time to do more of this! Any such thoughts are welcome to come and I'll immediately send them off and away.

I am dancing in Dr. Jamie Marich's session of Dancing Mindfulness, following her instructions the best I can: "There are no steps to follow… your body knows what to do… Mindfulness is noticing without judgment…"

When Jamie puts a slow piece on, my feet plant themselves in one spot. Now only my arms are dancing — slowly, as if delicately moving the air around me, and along with the air any feelings that are surfacing and radiating from me. I release tears that I didn't even know I was holding back, and my dance like a flow of water moves them in a circular motion until they all evaporate and lift up into the heavens like a weightless cloud.

WAKING UP FROM ADDICTION AND EMBRACING THE DANCE

Jamie was introduced to me when I was working on a charity project for Croatia. When I learned about our common roots, mentors and interests and watched her TEDx talk on trauma, I couldn't wait to interview her for *Waking Up in America*.

"Let's connect all the dots that bring us here today," I say excitedly as we sit down in her hotel suite in Nashville, Tennessee, and begin to unfurl what was to be a healing, life-shifting lesson.

Jamie was traveling through Europe after college as a backpacker, looking to meet people, learn about different cultures, and party. She only went to a small village and a pilgrimage destination in Bosnia and Herzegovina because her grandmother had always told her about it.

She ended up staying at Mother's Village for two years, teaching English and tutoring orphaned children at the a family-like community founded in 1993 during the war.

"I was on a very alcoholic path... [a] very destructive path at the time. Didn't know where I was going in life... Fr. Svet [a Franciscan priest who was in charge of Mother's Village at the time]... welcomed me to stay for an extended period and work teaching English..."

While there Jamie met an American social worker named Janet, who put her on the path of recovery.

But it was the children who ended up teaching Jamie about resilience and overcoming fear.

"It almost sounds cliché to say I found myself, but it really is what happened... for me travel is a medium that brings that out..."

She learned about the importance of faith in overcoming fear from a little girl named Anita, whom she taught how to ride a swing. When Anita fell off, Jamie let her cry and simply held her in her arms.

Before long Anita was back on the swing, declaring, "I'm not afraid any more."

"I was learning to live without alcohol; it became a matter of how do I address fear. How do I address feeling a heavy emotion? ... Seeing and hearing Anita having that experience... [it] really is about faith."

Jamie returned home to Youngstown, Ohio and, at the suggestion of both Janet and Fr. Svet, she got her doctorate in clinical counseling. She has published numerous books, operates a private practice and now travels internationally. Not only for enjoyment and leisure, but also to speak on topics related to EMDR (Eye Movement Desensitization and Reprocessing), trauma, addiction, and mindfulness.

I ask Jamie what her biggest joy in her work is and she takes a deep breath, closes her eyes and mindfully lets the answer come to her.

"Singing and dancing... Seeing somebody's soul start to sing, seeing somebody's soul start to dance... I can see that both when I teach and when I work with people... I can see that in my family and friends' connections often... I just love seeing people come to life."

And she adds, how often for our soul to start to sing, dance, and come to life, "a lot of tears need to be shed to take us there."

I make a circular motion with my hand to visually express this idea of a flow of tears and Jamie points out:

"[this motion, movement]... it's a river... it takes us to that journey where we need to go for healing... [it's] responding to the needs of the body."

This is what Jamie teaches in Dancing Mindfulness - both the practice and now the book.

Dancing Mindfulness comes from a combination of Jamie's passions: trauma work, using expressive arts for healing, meditation, and community gathering. Her love for dancing began when she was a little girl learning 'kolo,' traditional Croatian circle dances.

"Dancing Mindfulness is something we all do inherently. Because mindfulness is the art of being in the moment without judgment... and [dancing] has nothing to do with choreographed steps, or having to look a certain way. It's just moving the body with the sense of joy and freedom."

I think back on my childhood in Croatia and the endless weekends and family gatherings spent dancing, with grown-ups moving across the lawn, patio or even tiny kitchen floors, following the beat and laughing with abandonment.

"People have been doing this since the dawn of time..." Jamie says. Her contribution is in simply bringing it back and creating safe community spaces for it that are "trauma-informed, so you are not going to be judged for how you move..."

"Beautiful!" I exclaim, as the memory of those happy dances from my childhood also brings back images of drunken men behaving mindlessly, not mindfully. I like the idea of having a safe space to dance in.

Dancing Mindfulness is also a "legitimate form of meditation, a way to connect, center and pray," Jamie explains, and I take notice.

The day after my visit with Jamie and my experience in her class, I sit in my office. I put some music on and I get on my feet. I am alone in the house. For a moment I consider closing the shades in case my suburban neighbors glance in, but I let that thought pass. Mindfully. I lift up my arms and my feet begin to move. When the song ends, I feel refreshed, reconnected, and centered.

I send a wave of gratitude to Jamie, my friend who connected us, Fr. Svet, and all of the dots that connected to create this healing experience for me, and it forms into a prayer. As the prayer moves with and through my body, more tears come and take away whatever tension I was holding in. Like a river.

Like a dance.

Jamie Marich, PhD is a life-long dancer, the founder of Dancing Mindfulness, an author and a clinical counselor who leads trainings and retreats on trauma, addiction and mindfulness worldwide. Her newest book 'Dancing Mindfulness' is available on Amazon.com.

WATCH: Waking Up to Dance (with Dr. Jamie Marich) (EP 33)
LISTEN: "Breathe" (by Tajci)

PONDER: Dancing and mindfulness can both help in releasing blocks which prevent us from fully awakening.

APPLY: Turn on the music. Close the door. Stand in a spot where you can move freely without hurting yourself. Move your arms only at first if you are uncertain of this exercise… Bring your awareness to how you feel, what you are thinking. Dance and awaken.

CLOSING

*Every end
is a new beginning.*

MAKING BIG LIFE SHIFTS: IT'S NOT THAT SCARY AFTER YOU LEARN A FEW LESSONS FROM THOSE WHO HAVE DONE IT

Ask questions. Listen. Feel the gratitude.

EVERY BIG CHANGE IN OUR LIVES STARTS FROM WITHIN. Every transformation begins with an internal change, shift or intention before it manifests itself in our external reality — like starting a relationship, getting married, becoming a parent, pursuing a career or following a calling.

Some changes and transformations that we desire don't happen easily. Like diets we'd like to get on (and stay on) in order to improve our health, or addictions we know we need to quit, or careers we want to switch in order to free up time to spend with those we love.

For those transformations, we often need an external trigger. Something to whip us out from the spinning platforms of the proverbial carousels of our lives, which we've allowed to become the safe, familiar, pretty and closed cycle that keeps us stuck.

We often hear stories of such changes being triggered by traumatic events: switching to a healthy diet after an illness, starting recovery after hitting the rock bottom, or prioritizing how we spend our time after losing a loved one.

But why wait for such painful triggers?

Why not use the gentle ones available to us all the time?

For example, Thanksgiving is a great external opportunity for evaluating where we are, where we want to be, how much we have grown, and what we are holding onto that we still need to let go. The heightened presence of gratitude in the air can be a great "force field" to use when we confront ourselves and our goals. Because instead of disappointing and berating ourselves for our failures, we have the opportunity to shift into examining our lives from the perspective of gratitude.

Then there is the turn of the calendar year. Throwing out the old calendar and replacing it with a shiny new one can serve as a great external trigger. We start fresh, with lots of white space to fill with the pictures and words we want to see as a part of our story.

But the coolest part of 'starting fresh' is that we don't need to wait till Thanksgiving or January 1st, or any other 'special occasion' to use this external trigger — we can start right now.

Stories of those who have made significant shifts in their lives can help us in this process.

Over the past year I've interviewed 32 guests about turning points in various aspects of their lives on my show *Waking Up in America*.

Many of them had *clear* life-altering events that caused them to change their behaviors and thought patterns. For some it was a *series* of external triggers that finally awoke them, while for a few they were able to listen to that *whisper* deep within their soul and avoid a loud wake-up call.

I hope this book has inspired you to reflect on your own turning points and transformations.

Please share your story with us. Remember, you are not alone on your journey of transformation. We are here to support you.

Visit WakingUPrevolution.com for links to our internet and in-person events, groups and communities.

With gratitude,
Tajci

In Franklin, Tennessee on January 17th, 2016.

ALSO BY TAJCI

5 Step Guide eBook with graphics, links and worksheets.

CD with Tajci's original songs about awakening and relationships.

Available on Amazon.com
and
the Waking UP Store
at WakingUPrevolution.com

ABOUT THE AUTHOR

Tajci Cameron blogs on Huffington Post and writes stories and music. She is a rockstar mom, motivational speaker, Holistic Life Coach certified through Radiant Health Institute, published author and the host of the TV show *Waking Up in America*.

Having enjoyed two careers, one as a teenage pop superstar in Croatia and the other as a touring musician and completing a series of 1,000 performances, Tajci founded Waking UP Revolution, helping people to transform their personal and professional lives.

Tajci lives in Franklin, Tennessee with her husband and their three sons.

Tajci.net
WakingUPrevolution.com

#wakingUPrevolution

Made in the USA
Charleston, SC
11 June 2016